The Splitting Image

Exposing the Secret World of Doubles, Decoys, and Impostor-Replacements

Tina Foster

First Edition

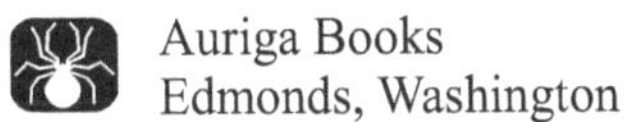

Auriga Books
Edmonds, Washington

Foster, Tina. *The Splitting Image: Exposing the Secret World of Doubles, Decoys, and Impostor-Replacements.*

ISBN-13: 9781795686815

Published in the United States by
Auriga Books
Edmonds, WA 98020
www.cynthiahodges.com/auriga

Contents

About the Author

Attorney and author, Tina Foster, has researched the area of doubles and imposter-replacements since 2008. Tina has examined how they are used in psy-ops by counter-intelligence, military, and the entertainment industry. Recognized as an authority on the subject, Tina has been invited to speak on radio shows in the USA, UK, Canada, and Australia. Tina's blog is Plastic Macca ~ Paul is Dead (plasticmacca.blogspot.com).

In this book, psychological operations involving doubles are explored. Politicians, heads of state, and other public figures routinely use doubles for a variety of clandestine purposes. Some are for security, while others serve more nefarious objectives. Political agendas can be promoted through the use of controlled doubles, for instance. Psy-ops using doubles are facilitated by means of technology, but technology can also be used to expose an impostor. Examples of historical doubles are discussed to illustrate certain tactical uses of lookalikes. Although some of the information may be disturbing, it leads to a greater understanding of how unseen forces operate in secret to manipulate perceptions and manage the populace.

Tina is also the author of *Plastic Macca: The Secret Death and Replacement of Beatle Paul McCartney,* available at amazon.com.

1. <u>Introduction</u>

The eye sees only what the
mind is prepared to comprehend.
~ Henri L. Bergson ~

    Former *Saturday Night Live* comedian, Tony Rosato, was imprisoned in 2005 after complaining to police that his wife and infant daughter had been replaced by impostors.[1] The prison psychiatrist, Dr. Duncan Scott, diagnosed Rosato with Capgras Syndrome, which is a mental illness characterized by the notion that someone has been replaced by a double.[2] Although Rosato's belief might seem funny on its face, the fact is that there is a long history of body doubles being used in psychological operations ("psy-ops"). Psy-ops are military operations "aimed at influencing the enemy's state of mind through noncombative means."[3] Public ignorance of how doubles are used in spycraft has helped to keep this realm of covert intelligence operations sub rosa. To protect the secret and keep the public in the dark, claims of doubles are ridiculed, denied, and suppressed by the powers that be.[4]

---

[1] Freed, Dale Anne. "From jokester to jailbird." Toronto Star Thestar.com. N.p., 13 May 2007. Web. 30 Dec. 2016. <http://www.thestar.com/News/article/213298>.

[2] *Id.*

[3] "Definition of psyops," Merriam-webster.com. Web. 13 Jan. 2017. <https://www.merriam-webster.com/dictionary/psyops>.

[4] *See* Beter, Dr. Peter David. "Audio Letter No. 46." May 28, 1979, <http://www.peterdavidbeter.com/docs/all/dbal46.html>.

Impostors have been used at least since medieval times to serve as instruments of intrigue.[5] Mata Hari, the famous World War I dancer and double agent, is an example. When she went to Berlin for espionage training, the Germans sent an impostor to take her place on her dancing tours.[6] No one noticed the difference.[7]

A double pretends to be someone else (the "target") in order to deceive onlookers into believing he is the other person. To be convincing, there must be a strong physical resemblance, which can be enhanced through the use of disguises, prosthetics, and plastic surgery. Identical twins are ideal doubles, because they are physically indistinguishable from one another. Antonio and Patricio de la Guardia were identical twin brothers who worked as Cuban spies.[8] Dr. Peter David Beter, intelligence specialist and author of the book *Conspiracy Against the Dollar*, maintained that clones, organic robotoids, and synthetic humans were being used as doubles in the late 1970's.[9] Fleshing out this possibility is beyond the scope of this book. Suffice it to say that anyone or *anything* could potentially serve as a double.

In addition to looking like his target, a double must speak and act like him. For example, former Prime Minister of the United Kingdom, Winston Churchill, was famous for the

---

[5] Beter, Dr. Peter David. "Audio Letter No. 44." N.p. 29 March 1979. Web. 30 Dec. 2016. <http://www.peterdavidbeter.com/docs/all/dbal44.html>.

[6] Armstrong, John. "JFK 101: An excerpt from 'Harvey & Lee: How the CIA Framed Oswald.'" Web. 30 Dec. 2016. <http://web.archive.org/web/20110404121334/http://www.jfkresearch.com/jfk_101.html>.

[7] *Id.*

[8] *Id.*

[9] Beter. "Audio Letter No. 46."

inspiring radio speeches he gave during World War II. However, some of those speeches were actually delivered by his voice double, Norman Shelley. [10]

Hillary Clinton, 2009[11]

One may think it difficult to find doubles for public figures. However, it is actually pretty easy. There are many talent agencies that specialize in lookalikes of celebrities and politicians. For example, Teresa Barnwell is a well-known impersonator of former Senator Hillary Clinton.[12] Even finding doubles to use as political decoys and in spycraft is not as difficult as one might assume. According to Antonio Mendez, former chief of disguise for the Central Intelligence Agency (CIA) and a co-author of the book *Spy Dust*, "Finding lookalikes willing to serve a higher calling isn't difficult, particularly when patriotic

---

[10] Thorpe, Vanessa. "Finest hour for actor who was Churchill's radio voice." The Observer. Guardian News and Media. N.p. 29 Oct. 2000. Web. 30 Dec. 2016. <https://www.theguardian.com/media/2000/oct/29/uknews.theobserver>.

[11] Photo by United States Department of State - Official Photo at Department of State page, Public Domain, https:/commons.wikimedia.org/w/index.php?curid=7526134.

[12] Kitching, Chris. "Is this the greatest Hillary lookalike in the world? Advertising executive quit her job to impersonate the presidential candidate full-time." Daily Mail. N.p. 11 July 2016. Web. 7 Jan. 2017. <http://www.dailymail.co.uk/news/article-3684267/Hillary-Clinton-lookalike-Teresa-Barnwell-quit-job-impersonate-presidential-candidate-time.html>.

passions are inflamed."[13] Some coercion may be necessary on occasion. Abdul-Latif Yahia agreed to work as Uday Hussein's double after being imprisoned and threatened with the rape of his sister.[14]

A South Korean actor, Kim Young-Shik, was cast in a movie role as former North Korean leader, Kim Jong-Il, because of his resemblance and ability to impersonate the "Dear Leader."[15] However, other actors may have played the role of Kim as doubles in real life.[16] According to North Korean refugees, there were several Kim lookalikes.[17] Ha Tae-kyung, host of Open Radio for North Korea, said a North

[13] Zeller, Tom. "The World; Will the Real Saddam Hussein Please Step Down." The New York Times. N.p. 6 Oct. 2002. Web. 30 Dec. 2016. <http://www.nytimes.com/2002/10/06/weekinreview/the-world-will-the-real-saddam-hussein-please-step-down.html>.

[14] Copel, Lib. "Body Double: Both Sides Of the Ploy." The Washington Post. N.p. 21 March 2003. Web. 13 Jan. 2017. <https://www.washingtonpost.com/archive/lifestyle/2003/03/21/body-double-both-sides-of-the-ploy/8352f20e-2836-4896-891c-c686d8cd00de/>.

[15] Jie-Ae, Sohn. "Meet Kim Jong Il's lookalike." CNN. Cable News Network. N.p. 7 Sept. 2006. Web. 30 Dec. 2016. <http://edition.cnn.com/2006/WORLD/asiapcf/09/07/kim.lookalike/index.html>; Demick, Barbara. "A Dictator's Double Is Keeping Up Appearances." Los Angeles Times. N.p. 11 June 2006. Web. 30 Dec. 2016. <http://articles.latimes.com/2006/jun/11/world/fg-lookalike11/2>.

[16] Kirk, Donald. "Would the real Kim Jong-Il please sit back down in his wheelchair?" WorldTribune.com. N.p. 30 Oct. 2009. Web. 30 Dec. 2016. <http://www.worldtribune.com/worldtribune/WTARC/2009/ea_nkorea0848_10_30.asp>.

[17] Kirk, Donald. "Did President Clinton meet N. Korea's Kim Jong-il or his look-alike?" The Christian Science Monitor. N.p. 29 Oct. 2009. Web. 30 Dec. 2016. <http://www.csmonitor.com/World/Asia-Pacific/2009/1029/p06s10-woap.html>.

Korean defector told him that "he [knew] a girl whose father [was] the actor for Kim Jong-Il."[18]

General Bernard Montgomery (left)[19] vs.
M.E. Clifton James (right)[20]

Meyrick Edward Clifton James, a British soldier and actor during World War II, landed the role of a lifetime when he was recruited to play the part of General Bernard Montgomery by United Kingdom Security Service, MI5.[21] James' uncanny resemblance to "Monty" was spotted by

18 Kirk. "Would the real Kim Jong-Il please sit back down in his wheelchair?"

19 Photo by http://www.maxwell.af.mil/au/afhra/wwwroot/photo_galleries/merhar/Photos/01097635_017.jpg, Public Domain, https://commons.wikimedia.org/w/index.php?curid=46423.

20 Photo by Unknown - Francis Russell: Wojna wywiadów, Warszawa, Amber 1998, ISBN 83-7169-748-1., Public Domain, https://commons.wikimedia.org/w/index.php?curid=24834791.

21 Hill, Martin. "The Imposter General: Bernard Montgomery's D-Day Body Double." Decoded Past. N.p. 15 June 2013. Web. 30 Dec. 2016. <http://decodedpast.com/the-imposter-general-bernard-montgomerys-d-day-body-double/1332>.

British Lieutenant-Colonel, J.V.B. Jervis-Reid in a 1944 newspaper article featuring James.[22] After the war, James recounted his experiences in his 1954 book, *I Was Monty's Double*.[23] In the 1958 film based on the book, James played both Montgomery and himself.[24]

Franklin D. Roosevelt may have had a double, as some researchers have noted the absence of a mole over his eyes and inconsistencies in the earlobes.[25] Some speculate that Roosevelt may have actually died before his death was officially announced.[26]

Former U.S. presidential candidate, Hillary Clinton, has been suspected of having a body double (other than Teresa Barnwell).[27] Photographs taken on September 11, 2016 purport to show differences in the cheekbones, skin (smooth versus wrinkled), and a different body type from previous

---

[22] Whaley, Barton and Susan Stratton Aykroyd. *Turnabout and Deception: Crafting the Double-Cross and the Theory of Outs*. Annapolis, MD: Naval Institute Press, 2016. p. 66.

[23] Hill. "The Imposter General: Bernard Montgomery's D-Day Body Double."

[24] *Id.*

[25] Springmeier, Fritz. *Deeper insight into the Illuminati Formula*. Charleston, SC: Createspace, 2010 p. 312. Print.

[26] *Id.*

[27] May, Ashley. "The Internet thinks Hillary Clinton has a body double." USA Today. N.p. 13 Sept. 2016. Web. 30 Dec. 2016. <http://www.usatoday.com/story/news/nation-now/2016/09/13/internet-thinks-hillary-clinton-has-body-double/90297312/>.

photos.[28] Some think the lack of security around Clinton that day was also a clue that a double was standing in for her.[29]

This book explores some tactical uses of doubles in psy-ops and discusses some of the more famous cases. Due to the furtive nature of clandestine operations, some of the allegations in this book are difficult to prove. The information is offered nonetheless to illustrate certain strategies involving doubles. In the interest of advancing historical doubles research, images of some of the people discussed in this book are available on the *Plastic Macca* blog at http://plasticmacca.blogspot.com/2017/01/the-splitting-image-by-tina-foster.html.

The next chapter deals with psychological warfare operations involving political decoys.

---

[28] *Id.*

[29] *Id.*

2. <u>Decoys</u>

I'm a substitute for another guy
I look pretty tall but my heels are high.
~ Peter Townsend ~

Doubles are indispensable to world leaders and the intelligence apparata surrounding them.[30] Hillary Clinton once joked that her lookalike, Teresa Barnwell, "could go to all the functions she didn't want to attend."[31] However, politicians actually do use doubles in public. A double's likeness to the target can make it seem as though an individual is in two places at once. This effect is referred to as "bilocation," and can be exploited for various purposes, especially security and counter-intelligence. Antonio Mendez said, "The idea of bilocation - of being able to be in two places at once - is key to some situations of security, Everyone uses it."[32]

Decoys are doubles that are used to improve security by thwarting assassination attempts, for counter-intelligence purposes, and to otherwise deceive potential enemies, such as leading spies down a false trail.[33] Choi Jin-Wook, a specialist at the Korea Institute of National Reunification, said that

---

[30] Zeller. "The World; Will the Real Saddam Hussein Please Step Down."

[31] Kitching. "Is this the greatest Hillary lookalike in the world? Advertising executive quit her job to impersonate the presidential candidate full-time."

[32] Zeller. "The World; Will the Real Saddam Hussein Please Step Down."

[33] Cornwell, Rupert. "The Kim Jong-il that Clinton met was a fake, says academic." The Independent. N.p. 31 Oct. 2009. Web. 30 Dec. 2016. <http://www.independent.co.uk/news/world/asia/the-kim-jongil-that-clinton-met-was-a-fake-says-academic-1812286.html>.

"dictators always need lookalikes for national security reasons."[34] Yahia, Uday Hussein's decoy, managed to survive numerous assassination attempts on Uday's life.[35]

Former Russian dictator, Joseph Stalin, was afraid of being assassinated, so he used decoys.[36] The doubles not only improved security, they also protected him from the many spies that surrounded him.[37] When Stalin travelled, four doubles would stand in for him on trips to the airport to throw spies off of his trail.[38] Nadezhda Nikolayevna, the daughter of General Nikolai Vlasik - head of Stalin's personal security - admitted, "[T]hey used doubles. All the tricks to distract attention from the leader were invented by my father."[39]

---

[34] Choi said that in reference to Kim Jong Il and Saddam Hussein. *Id.*

[35] Copel. "Body Double: Both Sides Of the Ploy."

[36] Stewart, Will. "The man who was Stalin's body double finally tells his story." Daily Mail Online. N.p. 12 April 2008.. Web. 30 Dec. 2016. <http://www.dailymail.co.uk/news/article-559234/The-man-Stalins-body-double-finally-tells-story.html>.

[37] *Id.*

[38] *Id.*

[39] *Id.*

Felix Dadaev (left) vs. Joseph Stalin (right)

Felix Dadaev was one of Stalin's doubles. The People's Commissariat of Internal Affairs (NKVD), the predecessor of the KGB (the Soviet Union's intelligence and internal security agency), ordered Dadaev to work as Stalin's double in 1943.[40] Dadaev took Stalin's place in motorcades, at rallies, and on newsreel footage.[41] Dadaev said, "Everyone was sure it was Stalin himself. I walked to the mausoleum with members of the government, then stood on the central dais, smiling and greeting the passing columns."[42]

A man known simply as "Rashid" was another one of Stalin's doubles. Rashid was twenty years younger than Stalin, but the likeness was so close that even his facial scars almost

---

[40] *Id.*

[41] *Id.*

[42] *Id.*

matched Stalin's smallpox pockmarks.[43] During World War II, Rashid's striking resemblance to the Soviet dictator came to the attention of the KGB.[44] They used Rashid to improve security by having him sit in for Stalin at meetings and banquets.[45]

Sir Winston Churchill, 1942

Winston Churchill, concerned about being killed by Nazi spies, employed at least one body double (other than voice double, Norman Shelley) as a security measure.[46] The stand-in would make personal appearances for the Prime Minister, and would even stay at Churchill's home.[47] This deception prevented the enemy from

---

[43] "Rashid, Josef Stalin's stand-in." Associated Press. St. Petersburg Times. 17 June 1991 (7B).

[44] *Id.*

[45] *Id.*

[46] Kurtus, Ron. "Winston Churchill: Final Years (Ages 70 - 90)." School for Champions. N.p. 6 Feb. 2006. Web. 31 Dec. 2016. <http://www.school-for-champions.com/biographies/winston_churchill_4.htm>.

[47] *Id.*

ever being certain as to Churchill's true whereabouts, which was meant to hinder any assassination attempts.[48]

MI5 exploited M. E. Clifton James' uncanny resemblance to General Montgomery for counter-intelligence purposes. James was part of a disinformation campaign regarding the Allies' plans to invade France during World War II. MI5 hoped to trick the Germans into believing that an Allied invasion would occur in southern France, and not in the north, where it was really planned.[49] James posed as Monty in Gibraltar and Algiers in 1944, where he dropped hints about "Plan 303," a phony plan to invade southern France.[50] The Allies' deception worked. Field Marshal Erwin Rommel's confidence in the intelligence he was receiving was shaken.[51] As a result, the German response to the Normandy Invasion was indecisive, which gave the Allies the advantage they needed for victory.[52]

Nazi dictator, Adolf Hitler, also had at least one double (identified as Gustav Weler), but he may have had as many as six.[53] The doubles would act as decoys at public events where Hitler's life may have been in danger.

---

[48] *Id.*

[49] Hill. "The Imposter General: Bernard Montgomery's D-Day Body Double."

[50] *Id.*

[51] "Psychological Warfare." Allexperts. com. Web. 30 Dec. 2016. <http://web.archive.org/web/20080709014354/http://en.allexperts.com/e/p/ps/psychological_warfare.htm>.

[52] "Psychological Warfare."

[53] Dean, Bradlee. "Politicians' Body Doubles Nothing New." WND. N.p. 15 Sept. 2016. Web. 30 Dec. 2016. <http://www.wnd.com/2016/09/politicians-body-doubles-nothing-new/>.

Federal Bureau of Investigations (FBI) files uncovered by a team of former CIA investigators proved Hitler used a double to fake his death and escape to Argentina.[54] The "Hitler" corpse the Russians found after Hitler's alleged suicide on April 30, 1945 was five inches shorter than Hitler and had a smaller skull.[55] DNA analysis also proved "Hitler's skull" was actually from a woman between the ages of twenty and forty (Hitler was fifty-six).[56] Journalist, author and historian, Gerrard Williams, claims that two body doubles for Hitler and Eva Braun were murdered as part of the plan.[57] The unfortunate victims served as decoys, allowing the real Hitler and Braun to flee Berlin.

---

[54] Mansfield, Katie. "Secret FBI files 'reveal Hitler DID fake death' after WW2 then flew to TENERIFE" Daily Express. N.p. 8 Jan. 2016. Web. 31 Dec. 2016. <http://www.express.co.uk/news/weird/632677/Adolf-Hitler-Nazi-fake-death-World-War-Two-Tenerife>.

[55] Id.

[56] Goñi, Uki. "Tests on skull fragment cast doubt on Adolf Hitler suicide story." The Guardian. N.p. 26 Sept. 2009. Web. 15 Jan. 2017. <https://www.theguardian.com/world/2009/sep/27/adolf-hitler-suicide-skull-fragment>.

[57] Rao, Nathan. "Hitler DID escape Germany in 1945: Staggering new claims point to huge Nazi cover-up." Daily Express. N.p. 12 June 2015. Web. 31 Dec. 2016. <http://www.express.co.uk/news/weird/583845/Did-Hitler-ESCAPE-Germany-in-1945-Staggering-new-discovery-points-to-huge-Nazi-cover-up>.

Saddam Hussein: 1979 (left)[58] vs. 2003 (right)[59]

Former Iraqi president, Saddam Hussein, routinely used doubles as decoys to take his place on T.V. and in public appearances.[60] He did this to hide his true whereabouts and to

---

[58] Photo by INA (Iraqi News Agency) - Dar al-Ma'mun, Public Domain, https://commons.wikimedia.org/w/index.php?curid=31285998.

[59] Photo by US DoD Photo - http://www.dodmedia.osd.mil/DVIC_View/ Still_Details.cfm?SDAN=DDSD0501885&JPGPath=/Assets/2005/DoD/ DD-SD-05-01885.JPG, Public Domain, https://commons.wikimedia.org/w/ index.php?curid=1504832.

[60] "Austria's Haider Met Saddam Lookalike--Report." Reuters, N.p. 6 Oct. 2002, Web. 31 Dec. 2016. <http://web.archive.org/web/20110713071007/ h t t p : / / n e w s 1 . i w o n . c o m / o d d / a r t i c l e / i d / 272230%7Coddlyenough%7C10-06-2002::12:01%7Creuters.html>; Zeller. "The World; Will the Real Saddam Hussein Please Step Down."

thwart his enemies.[61] The real Hussein did not appear in public from 1998 until September 21, 2002.[62] Austrian right-wing politician, Joerg Haider, met with one of Hussein's doubles in February 2002.[63] Dr. Dieter Buhmann, a German pathologist at the Institute of Forensic Medicine at Homberg University, explained that, "Despite a certain likeness (to Hussein), there are... differences, thanks to which one can exclude the possibility that this was the real Saddam."[64]

Dr. Buhmann found that Saddam Hussein had used at least three doubles.[65] Other sources, including Western and Arab intelligence agencies, maintained that Hussein had as

[61] Morales, Tatiana. "CIA: Man On Tape Is Saddam." CBS News. N.p. 21 March 2003. Web. 30 Dec. 2016. <http://www.cbsnews.com/stories/2003/03/20/eveningnews/main544812.shtml>.; Recknagel, Charles. "Iraq: Seeing Double In Baghdad -- Saddam Uses Look-Alikes To Disguise His Whereabouts." Radio Free Europe/Radio Liberty. N.p. 9 Oct. 2002. Web. 31 Dec. 2016. <http://www.rferl.org/content/article/1101033.html>

[62] Recknagel. "Iraq: Seeing Double In Baghdad -- Saddam Uses Look-Alikes To Disguise His Whereabouts."

[63] "Austria's Haider Met Saddam Lookalike--Report."

[64] Recknagel. "Iraq: Seeing Double In Baghdad -- Saddam Uses Look-Alikes To Disguise His Whereabouts."; Cienfuegos, Ernesto, "Iraqi Resistance Stiffens Amidst Claims Saddam's Capture was a Hoax." La Voz de Aztlan. N.p. 16 Dec. 2003. Web. 31 Dec. 2016. <http://web.archive.org/web/20031221100907/http://www.aztlan.net/saddamcapturehoax.htm>; Morales. "CIA: Man On Tape Is Saddam."; "Austria's Haider Met Saddam Lookalike--Report."

[65] McWethy, John, Brian Ross, Pierre Thomas and Martha Raddatz. "Saddam Hit? U.S.: Saddam Seen Leaving Baghdad Complex on a Gurney After Strike." ABC News. N.p. 21 March 2003. Web. 31 Dec. 2016. <http://web.archive.org/web/20030324225555/http://abcnews.go.com/sections/world/World/iraq_saddam_030321.html>.

many as thirteen doubles.[66] The names of three of the doubles have been identified: Hatem El-A'aly, Fawzy El-Emary (or Faoas al-Emari) and Mikhail Ramadan.[67]

John Perkins, author of Confessions of an Economic Hitman, wrote that Hussein's doubles protected him from CIA Jackals who were trying to assassinate him.[68] In 1984, the Shiite Dawa actually did kill one of Hussein's decoys by mistake.[69]

Kim Jong Il was afraid of being assassinated in a coup d'état, so he used at least four doubles to substitute for him at public events, outside ceremonies, and while traveling around North Korea.[70] Toshimitsu Shigemura, Professor of International Relations at Tokyo's Waseda University and author of The True Character of Kim Jong Il, cited three

---

[66] El Mallah, Yasmeen, "Anis El-Dighidy." Egypt Today. N.p. May 2007. Web. 31 Dec. 2016. <http://web.archive.org/web/20070516071840/http://www.egypttoday.com/article.aspx?ArticleID=7376>.

[67] Pelton, Robert Young. "Iraq - President Saddam Hussein al-Tikriti." N.p. 2000. Web. 31 Dec. 2016. <http://web.archive.org/web/20010504000910/http://www.comebackalive.com/df/dplaces/iraq/player5.htm>; El Mallah, "Anis El-Dighidy."

[68] "Confessions of an Economic Hit Man: How the U.S. Uses Globalization to Cheat Poor Countries Out of Trillions." Democracy Now! N.p. 9 Nov. 2004. Web. 31 Dec. 2016. <https://www.democracynow.org/2004/11/9/confessions_of_an_economic_hit_man>.

[69] Pelton. "Iraq - President Saddam Hussein al-Tikriti."

[70] Ryall, Julian. "Kim Jong-Il 'died in 2003', says Japanese professor." The Telegraph. 7 Sept. 2008. Web. 31 Dec. 2016. <http://www.telegraph.co.uk/news/2699670/Kim-Jong-Il-died-in-2003-says-Japanese-professor.html>; Sheridan, Michael. "North Korea 'uses doubles to hide death of Kim.'" The Sunday Times. N.p. 7 Sept. 2008. Web. 31 Dec. 2016. <http://web.archive.org/web/20080911065831/http://www.timesonline.co.uk/tol/news/world/asia/article4692472.ece>; Kirk. "Would the real Kim Jong-Il please sit back down in his wheelchair?"

Japanese sources who claimed to have met Kim's doubles.[71] One even admitted to being one of the stand-ins.[72] A North Korean agent also claimed to have met one of Kim's lookalikes.[73]

This chapter explained how decoys can be used for security and counter-intelligence purposes. In the next chapter, using doubles to set up alibis and patsies will be discussed.

---

[71] Kirk. "Did President Clinton meet N. Korea's Kim Jong-il or his look-alike?"

[72] *Id.*

[73] Ryall. "Kim Jong-Il 'died in 2003', says Japanese professor."

3. <u>Alibis and Patsies</u>

I'm just a patsy.
~ Lee Harvey Oswald ~

In addition to the obvious counter-intelligence uses, doubles can serve more nefarious purposes. In the context of espionage or in the commission of a crime, *Doppelgängers* can be used to create an alibi or frame a patsy. A patsy is the hapless victim set up to take the blame for a crime.

To create an alibi, two lookalikes could be used. One would be involved in committing the illegal or clandestine act, while the other would be somewhere else with people who could provide an alibi for him.[74] If the person committing the act of espionage or crime were identified, he could simply give the authorities the names of the people who were with his lookalike.[75] Those witnesses would verify his alibi, so he would more than likely be cleared as a suspect.[76] If the authorities had no knowledge of his double, he would probably not be charged with a crime.[77] In a professional and carefully planned operation, no one would know about the double, so both individuals involved would walk away scot-free.[78]

---

[74] Armstrong. "JFK 101: An excerpt from 'Harvey & Lee: How the CIA Framed Oswald.'"

[75] *Id.*

[76] *Id.*

[77] *Id.*

[78] *Id.*

Sometimes, a criminal's clever use of a double to establish an alibi fails. On April 26, 2010, Venus Stewart was kidnapped and murdered in Michigan.[79] Her estranged husband, Douglas Stewart, was the chief suspect.[80] However, he was seen by multiple witnesses in Virginia at the time of the incident.[81] Once police obtained proof that Stewart was in Michigan at the time of the crime, they charged him with kidnapping and murder.[82] Investigators figured out that Stewart had convinced an impostor, Richard Spencer, to create an alibi for him by making public appearances in Virginia during the time the crime was being committed in Michigan.[83]

Setting up a patsy could also involve the use of a double. In such an operation, a patsy would be chosen to take the blame for a criminal act. A lookalike of the patsy would commit the crime, and any witnesses would identify the patsy as the culprit.[84] Upon arrest, the patsy could deny any involvement in the crime, but the authorities would probably not believe him.[85] He would then take the fall while the real perpetrator would escape justice.

---

[79] Kotz, Pete. "Douglas Stewart Used Impostor to Derail Cops in Disappearance of Wife Venus Stewart." True Crime Report. N.p. 24 June 2010. Web. 11 Jan. 2017. <http://www.truecrimereport.com/2010/06/douglas_stewart_used_imposter.php>.

[80] *Id.*

[81] *Id.*

[82] *Id.*

[83] *Id.*

[84] Armstrong. "JFK 101: An excerpt from 'Harvey & Lee: How the CIA Framed Oswald.'"

[85] *Id.*

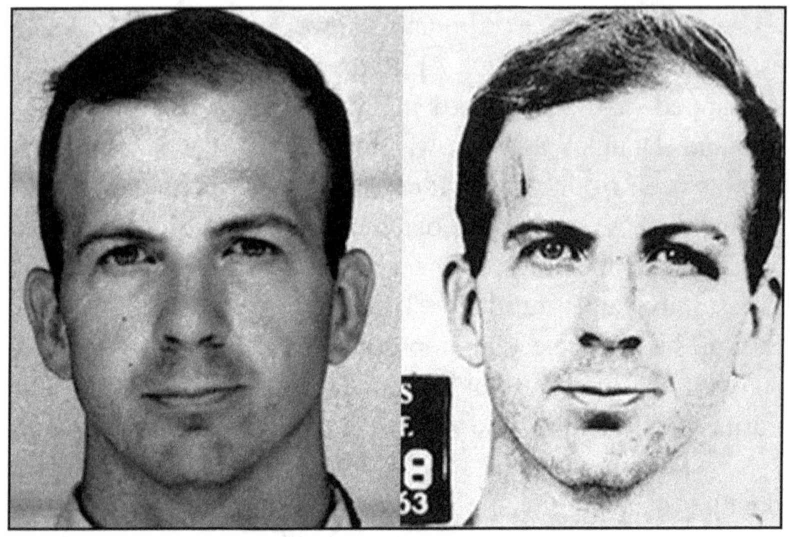

Lee Harvey Oswald: New Orleans, 9 Aug. 1963 (left) vs. Dallas, 22 Nov. 1963 (right)

Lee Harvey Oswald claimed to be a patsy when he was arrested for shooting President John F. Kennedy and Officer J. D. Tippit on November 22, 1963. John Armstrong, author of *Harvey and Lee: How the CIA Framed Oswald*, speculated that conspirators had used a double to set up Oswald as a patsy.[86] Prior to that fateful day, there had been many unusual sightings of Oswald all over Dallas. In one case, a used car salesman reported that "Lee Oswald" had test driven a Cadillac at speeds of up to 70 miles per hour, but Oswald did not know how to drive and was at home at the time.[87] Other

[86] Hildebrand, Holly. "The Mystery of Lee Harvey Oswald." The Houston Chronicle. N.p. 22 April 2000. Web. 30 Dec. 2016. <http://web.archive.org/web/20000422222051/http://www.chron.com/content/chronicle/special/jfk/theory/oswald.html>.

[87] *Id.*; "Interview with the Assassin: Misinformaton." Magnolia Pictures. Web. 30 Dec. 2016. <http://web.archive.org/web/20021003185303/http://www.interviewwiththeassassin.com/misinformation.html>.

witnesses were certain they had seen Oswald at a barber shop, a furniture store, a gun shop, and a grocery store, but Oswald was known to have been somewhere else in all of those instances.[88] As CIA official, "John Scelso," put it, "Dozens of people were claiming that they had seen Oswald here, there, and everywhere... from the North Pole to the Congo."[89]

At the time of both the Kennedy and Tippit murders, witness testimony placed Oswald in different places (bilocation). The Warren Commission found that Oswald had fired the fatal shots at Kennedy from the sixth floor of the Texas School Book Depository (TSBD) in Dallas, Texas.[90] Kennedy's motorcade had been scheduled to pass the TSBD at about 12:25 pm.[91] Ten witnesses noticed suspicious activity on an upper floor of the TSBD from about 12:15 pm until the shooting at 12:30 pm.[92] Six witnesses saw a gunman on the sixth floor during the actual assassination.[93] Only one, Charles Givens, testified that he had seen Oswald there at 11:55 pm.[94] However, Givens had told the FBI earlier that he had seen

---

[88] Hildebrand. "The Mystery of Lee Harvey Oswald,"

[89] "Scelso," John. "HSCA Security Classified Testimony: 1-173." 16 May 1978. Web. 30 Dec. 2016. <http://www.history-matters.com/archive/jfk/hsca/secclass/Scelso_5-16-78/html/Scelso_0177a.htm>.

[90] "JFK Assassination Records: Findings." National Archives. Web. 11 Jan. 2017. <https://www.archives.gov/research/jfk/select-committee-report/part-1a.html>.

[91] "Who Saw Lee Harvey Oswald in the TSBD Sixth-Floor Window?" 22november1963.org.uk. Web. 10 Jan. 2017. <http://22november1963.org.uk/who-saw-oswald-in-the-sixth-floor-window>.

[92] *Id.*

[93] *Id.*

[94] *Id.*

Oswald on the first floor of TSBD at that time.[95] The other witnesses gave descriptions of the gunman that *could* have been Oswald. Howard Brennan said that he saw "a white man in his early 30's, slender, nice looking, and would weigh about 165 to 175 pounds" and was five feet ten inches tall.[96] Arnold Rowland and Ronald Fischer both described the gunman as "slender," and Fischer said that "he looked to be 22 or 24 years old."[97] Oswald was white, slender, 24 years old, five feet nine or ten inches tall, and weighed 131 pounds.[98] Robert Edwards said that the gunman's hair was "light brown" and Carolyn Walther remembered "blond or light brown hair."[99] Oswald's hair was light brown, and receding slightly.[100] However, Arnold Rowland said the man he saw on the sixth floor with a rifle at 12:15 pm had "dark hair... probably black... It didn't appear as if he had a receding hairline."[101] Amos Euins saw "a bald spot on this man's head, trying to look out the window."[102] However, Oswald did not have a bald spot.[103]

---

[95] *Id.*

[96] *Id.*

[97] *Id.*

[98] *Id.*

[99] *Id.*

[100] *Id.*

[101] *Citing* Warren Commission Hearings, vol.2, pp.171–3. *Id.*

[102] "Who Saw Lee Harvey Oswald in the TSBD Sixth-Floor Window?"

[103] *Id.*

Oswald gave an alibi to FBI agents, James Hosty and James Bookhout, saying he was "on the first floor when President John F. Kennedy passed this building."[104] He told Captain J.W. Fritz of the Dallas police "that he was having his lunch about that time on the first floor."[105] Carolyn Arnold corroborated Oswald's alibi, saying she saw him on either the first or second floor at around 12:15 pm.[106] At about 12:23 p.m., James Jarman and Harold Norman saw Oswald on the first floor.[107] Therefore, witnesses place Oswald on the first or second floor of the TSBD at the same time a lookalike gunman was preparing to shoot Kennedy on the sixth floor.

Forty to forty-five minutes after the Kennedy assassination, Helen Markham and Jack Tatum saw Oswald shoot Tippit.[108] William Scoggins, Barbara Davis, and Virginia Davis saw him flee the scene.[109] Ted Callaway, Sam Guinyard, B.M. Patterson, L.J. Lewis, Harold Russell, and Warren Reynolds "saw Oswald brandishing a pistol, attempting to conceal it, and fleeing the area."[110] However, another witness saw Oswald in the Texas Theater at the time as the shooting.

---

104 "What Was Lee Harvey Oswald's Alibi?" 22november1963.org.uk. Web. 10 Jan. 2017. <http://22november1963.org.uk/lee-harvey-oswald-alibi>.

105 *Id.*

106 *Id.*

107 *Id.*

108 "November 22: The Evidence." J.D. Tippett. Web. 9 Jan. 2017. <https://www.jdtippit.com/evidence_nov.htm>.

109 *Id.*

110 *Id.*

The Warren Commission concluded that Tippit was shot at 1:16 pm, but at 1:15 pm, Butch Burroughs sold Oswald popcorn at the Texas Theater.[111] If the Warren Commission's finding that Tippit was killed at 1:16 pm were correct, then Oswald was in the middle of a popcorn purchase.

There is some dispute as to the exact timing of the Tippit murder, however. The Dallas Police log put it at 1:10 pm.[112] If the police log were correct, then Oswald would not have been able to walk to the murder scene in time. At 1:03 pm, Earlene Roberts saw Oswald outside his rental room nine–tenths of a mile away from the crime scene.[113] The FBI and the Secret Service each took twelve minutes to walk from Oswald's location to the murder site.[114] It is highly unlikely Oswald could have walked to the Tippit murder scene in seven minutes to kill him by 1:10 pm. The Tippit shooter, then, was most likely an Oswald impersonator.

Another indication that an impostor framed Oswald was the brown wallet Dallas Police Captain Pinky Westbrook found at the scene of the Tippit shooting.[115] This wallet

---

[111] Armstrong, John. "Harvey, Lee and Tippit: A New Look at the Tippit Shooting." Kennedys and King. N.p. 15 Feb. 1998. Web. 9 Jan. 2017. <https://kennedysandking.com/john-f-kennedy-articles/harvey-lee-and-tippit-a-new-look-at-the-tippit-shooting>.

[112] *Id.*

[113] "Did Lee Harvey Oswald Kill J.D. Tippett?" 22November 1063. org.uk. Web. 9 Jan. 2017. <http://22november1963.org.uk/did-lee-harvey-oswald-kill-officer-jd-tippit>.

[114] *Id.*

[115] Armstrong. "Harvey, Lee and Tippit: A New Look at the Tippit Shooting."

contained Oswald's identification, and was probably planted there for police to find.[116]

As has been shown, doubles can assist in espionage and criminal activities. They can help the perpetrator escape justice by making it seem like he was somewhere else. A patsy can be made to seem like he was at the scene of the crime, even though he was not. Oswald was shot by Jack Ruby before he could give evidence to support his claim of being a patsy, or reveal what he knew about the conspiracy to kill Kennedy (or was he?)

President Kennedy was publicly executed to no doubt further *someone's* political agenda. The next chapter deals with heads of state who have died or been secretly killed and surreptitiously replaced by a double to further a political agenda.

---

[116] *Id.*

4. <u>The Replacements</u>

You can be replaced, Cheeky Baby!
~ From a scene in *A Hard Day's Night* (1964) ~

As has been shown, political leaders use doubles to deceive their enemies. However, two can play at that game. For example, a leader's opponents could stage a secret *coup d'état* by covertly eliminating him and replacing him with a convincing lookalike. The impostor would assume the leader's identity, position, power, and influence. The double would be able to "carry out official acts, give orders, and sign agreements."[117] The puppet double could then advance any political agenda his controllers wanted. "The whole empire could be taken over without eliminating anyone except the very closest associates of those who had secretly disappeared..."[118] The unsuspecting public would be none the wiser as to what was really happening behind the scenes.

Impostor-replacement has been a recurring theme in works of fiction dating back to at least 1847. In the novel, *The Man in the Iron Mask* by Alexandre Dumas, The Three Musketeers, Aramis, Athos and Porthos, tried to stage a *coup* by replacing King Louis XIV of France with his identical twin brother, Philippe. Aramis hoped Phillipe would further his political aspirations, namely to one day become Pope.[119]

---

117 Beter. "Audio Letter No. 46."

118 Beter. "Audio Letter No. 44."

119 May, Stephen. "The Top 10 Impostors in Fiction." The Guardian. N.p. 12 March 2014. Web. 2 Jan. 2017. <https://www.theguardian.com/books/2014/mar/12/top-10-impostors-fiction-stephen-may>.

Another fictional account of impostor-replacement occurred in the 1993 film, *Dave*, starring Kevin Kline. In this movie, an actor, "Dave," was hired to play the part of the ailing U.S. president. Dave was then manipulated by political insiders to serve their agenda.

Although the impostor-replacement scenario may seem far-fetched, according to Dr. Beter, "History is replete with the exploits of impostors who have taken the place of the rich and the powerful, and often they have been remarkably successful."[120] Even more surprisingly, Dr. Beter claimed that the Bolsheviks had staged a covert *coup d'etat* in the United States and were using doubles to secretly control the government.[121]

The Bolsheviks were the faction of the Russian Social-Democratic Workers' Party who, under the leadership of Vladimir Lenin, overthrew the Russian government in October 1917.[122] The Bolsheviks, proponents of Marxism (the antithesis of Capitalism), created an undemocratic and highly centralized form of government that suppressed all political rivals.[123] The Bolsheviks changed their name to the Communist Party of the Soviet Union in October 1952.[124]

Nikita Khrushchev, former Premier of the Soviet Union, once declared, "We do not have to invade the United

---

[120] Beter. "Audio Letter No. 44."

[121] Beter. "Audio Letter No. 46."

[122] "Bolshevik." Encyclopedia Britannica. Web. 17 Jan. 2017. <https://www.britannica.com/topic/Bolshevik>.

[123] *Id.*

[124] *Id.*

States, we will destroy you from within."[125] The secret Soviet *coup* in America supposedly began on January 26, 1979 when "Nelson Rockefeller was liquidated" and was over by February 17, 1979, when both David and Laurance Rockefeller had been executed.[126] Dr. Beter said he had intelligence that David Rockefeller, former President Jimmy Carter, and former Vice President Walter Mondale had been killed in the Bolshevik purge and replaced with controlled doubles.[127]

President Jimmy Carter, 31 Jan. 1977

David Rockefeller was allegedly killed on February 9, 1979.[128] A "very good" Bolshevik-controlled double started to appear in public at the end of February 1979.[129] Because David Rockefeller had been chairman and chief executive of the Chase-Manhattan Bank,

---

[125] "Nikita Khrushchev Quotes." Web. 17 Jan. 2017. <http://www.azquotes.com/author/7985-Nikita_Khrushchev>.

[126] Beter. "Audio Letter No. 44."

[127] *Id.*

[128] *Id.*

[129] *Id.*

the Bolsheviks were able to use the double to plunder the Rockefeller fortune, "eating away the assets of Chase-Manhattan Bank from within."[130]

President Carter, another purported victim of the Bolshevik *coup*, was shot in the head on April 21, 1979 in Plains, Georgia.[131] He is said to have died on April 22, 1979 at Bethesda Naval Hospital.[132] Carter was also replaced by a Bolshevik-controlled double, but this one looked and acted "ten years younger than the real Carter did."[133] In addition, Carter's "tired, halting voice" was replaced by a shrill voice that was "forceful, vigorous, and confident."[134]

Vice President Mondale was also ostensibly executed in the Bolshevik purge by a bullet to the brain.[135] This is said to have occurred in New Richmond, Wisconsin on April 20, 1979.[136] Mondale was also replaced by a Bolshevik-controlled puppet.[137]

Dr. Henry Kissinger, former National Security Advisor of the United States, was said to be a key player in the new Bolshevik regime and "was positioning himself to pick up the

---

[130] Beter. "Audio Letter No. 44."

[131] Beter, Dr. Peter David. "Audio Letter No. 45." N.p. 27 April 1979. Web. 6 Jan. 2017. <http://www.peterdavidbeter.com/docs/all/dbal45.html>.

[132] *Id.*

[133] *Id.*

[134] *Id.*

[135] *Id.*

[136] *Id.*

[137] *Id.*

reins of Rockefeller power."[138] However, on February 5, 1979, the private jet Kissinger was aboard supposedly exploded over the North Atlantic as it flew from London to the United States.[139] There were no survivors.[140] A tan Kissinger double turned up in Acapulco, Mexico, where Kissinger was said to be on vacation (a cover story concocted by the Bolsheviks to explain Kissinger's absence from the world stage).[141] It is possible that Kissinger was himself assassinated by the intelligence services in the power struggle that was occurring during the *coup*. At any rate, the Bolsheviks could still exploit Kissinger's position and influence by using a double, even if they had lost a key strategist.

"The war of 'doubles' involve[d] not only the Bolsheviks but the clandestine services of Russia, Great Britain and Israel; but the basic battle lines [were] being drawn between Russia and the Bolsheviks."[142] It is *possible*, then, that Vladimir Putin, president of the Russian Federation, countered the Bolsheviks when he was a Russian KGB foreign intelligence officer. Putin has publicly "denounced Lenin and his Bolshevik government for their brutal repressions..."[143] He

---

[138] Beter. "Audio Letter No. 44."

[139] *Id.*

[140] Dr. Beter said the jet crashed into the sea "at the navigational coordinates 54 degrees, 40 minutes, 57 seconds North; 26 degrees, 40 minutes, zero seconds West." *Id.*

[141] Beter. "Audio Letter No. 44."

[142] Beter. "Audio Letter No. 46."

[143] "Vladimir Putin accuses Lenin of placing a 'time bomb' under Russia." The Guardian. N.p. 25 Jan. 2016. Web. 17 Jan. 2017. <https://www.theguardian.com/world/2016/jan/25/vladimir-putin-accuses-lenin-of-placing-a-time-bomb-under-russia>.

has also spoken out against the Bolsheviks' "betrayal of the Russian national interests," and has actually accused Lenin of having been a traitor.[144]

Vladimir Putin: 23 April 2007 (left) vs. 27 March 2015 (right)[145]

Putin is himself suspected of having been impostor-replaced, because his face has changed dramatically when compared to pictures taken in his youth.[146] According to

---

[144] Lipman, Masha. "Putin Disses Lenin." The New Yorker. N.p. 3 Sept. 2014. Web. 17 Jan. 2017. <http://www.newyorker.com/news/news-desk/putin-disses-lenin>.

[145] Photo by Kremlin.ru, CC BY 4.0, https://commons.wikimedia.org/w/index.php?curid=40763566).

[146] O'Flynn, Elaine. "What has he been Putin on his face? How Russian leader Vladimir's appearance has changed dramatically through the years and he looks younger than ever." Daily Mail. N.p. 16 April 2015. Web. 1 Jan. 2017. <http://www.dailymail.co.uk/news/article-3042134/What-Putin-face-Russian-leader-Vladimirs-appearance-changed-dramatically-years-looks-younger-ever.html>.

historian Patrick Scrivener, the new Putin has a rounder head, a fatter, shorter nose, thicker lips, a larger mouth, a double chin, and a missing dimple.[147] In addition, wrinkles on his forehead, which were visible in previous pictures, have disappeared.[148] There are reports that Putin had plastic surgery, but that could just be a cover to explain the changes.[149]

There is no consensus among researchers about when Putin may have been replaced. Some say Putin was poisoned in the Kremlin after annexing Crimea in 2014 or killed by the CIA and MI6 (British Secret Intelligence Service), and replaced by a CIA controlled double.[150] Others believe Putin may have been replaced in a secret *coup d'état* in 2015.[151] They point to Putin's mysterious disappearance from public view from March 5 - 15, 2015 as evidence.[152] It is also possible that Putin was replaced much earlier, before he even ascended to the presidency.

Putin would not be the first Russian leader to have been suspected of having been impostor-replaced. Leonid Brezhnev (former General Secretary of the Central Committee

---

[147] Holloway, Henry. "'Putin is DEAD' Shock claims Vlad was killed YEARS ago and Russia led by 'body double.'" Daily Star Sunday. N.p. 24 Dec. 2016. Web. 1 Jan. 2017. <http://www.dailystar.co.uk/news/latest-news/572181/Vladimir-Putin-Russia-Body-Double-Dead-Poison-CIA-Mi6-Kremlin-US-Crimea>.

[148] O'Flynn. "What has he been Putin on his face? How Russian leader Vladimir's appearance has changed dramatically through the years and he looks younger than ever."

[149] Holloway. "'Putin is DEAD' Shock claims Vlad was killed YEARS ago and Russia led by 'body double.'"

[150] *Id.*

[151] *Id.*

[152] *Id.*

of the Communist Party of the Soviet Union) was said to have died in Moscow on January 7, 1978.[153] A few weeks later, a ceremonial Brezhnev double began taking his place at public functions.[154]

A similar scenario may have played out in North Korea. Professor Shigemura maintained that Kim Jong Il had died in the autumn of 2003 due to poor health.[155] (Kim's "official" date of death is December 17, 2011). Kim had suffered from "diabetes, heart disease, liver disorder, [and] lung problems..." (confirmed by South Korea's intelligence service, and Russian and Chinese sources).[156] After the inter-Korean summit with South Korea President Kim Dae-jung in June 2000, Kim Jong Il "was bedridden with diabetes" and confined to a wheelchair until his alleged death in 2003.[157]

---

[153] Beter, Dr. Peter David. "Audio Letter No. 33." N.p. 28 April 1978. Web. 30 Dec. 2016. <http://www.peterdavidbeter.com/docs/all/dbal33.html>.

[154] *Id.*

[155] Ryall. "Kim Jong-Il 'died in 2003', says Japanese professor."; Sheridan. "North Korea 'uses doubles to hide death of Kim.'"

[156] Takahashi, Kosuke. "Seeing Doubles in Dear Leader's No-Show," Asia Times. N.p. 10 Sept. 2008. Web. 31 Dec. 2016. <http://www.atimes.com/atimes/Korea/JI10Dg01.html>; Sheridan. "North Korea 'uses doubles to hide death of Kim.'"; Moore, Malcolm and Julian Ryall. "North Korea Denies Kim Jong-Il Dead and Claim 'Conspiracy.'" The Telegraph. N.p. 10 Sept. 2008. Web. 31 Dec. 2016. <http://www.telegraph.co.uk/news/2775598/North-Korea-deny-Kim-Jong-il-dead-and-claim-conspiracy.html>.

[157] Kirk. "Did President Clinton meet N. Korea's Kim Jong-il or his look-alike?"; Kuchikomi. "N Korea's Kim Died in 2003; Replaced by Lookalike, Says Waseda Professor." Japan Today. N.p. 23 Aug. 2008. Web. 31 Dec. 2016. <https://www.japantoday.com/category/kuchikomi/view/north-koreas-kim-died-in-2003-and-was-replaced-by-lookalike-says-waseda-profesor>.

After Kim's death, a series of doubles took his place at official state events.[158] The Kim family, the military and other top officials had a personal stake in the survival of the North Korean regime.[159] It is possible that Kim's early demise may have been concealed to avoid complications in the transition of power to Kim Jong-un.[160] It is also possible that a group of four senior military officials protected their own positions by making the Kim impostors permanent.[161] The doubles were trotted out whenever it was necessary to convince the public that Kim was still alive.[162] The four senior military figures shadowed the Kim doubles "like a puppet-master" whenever someone met with "Kim."[163]

Saddam Hussein is another leader suspected of having been impostor-replaced. Moslem Al-Asadi, a doctor living in exile in Iran, said, "The real Saddam died because he had cancer of the lymph nodes, and since his death in 1999, they're just showing his doubles."[164] A former bodyguard agreed, "Saddam whom you now see, was photographed some years

---

[158] Ryall. "Kim Jong-Il 'died in 2003', says Japanese professor."

[159] Branigan, Tania. "Kim Jong-il 'Has Pancreatic Cancer,'" The Guardian UK. N.p. 13 July 2009. Web. 31 Dec. 2016. <https://www.theguardian.com/world/2009/jul/13/kim-jong-il-cancer>.

[160] *Id.*

[161] Ryall. "Kim Jong-Il 'died in 2003', says Japanese professor."

[162] Sheridan. "North Korea 'uses doubles to hide death of Kim.'"

[163] Barlow, Karen. "Kim Jong-Il 'died in 2003.'" ABC News. N.p. 7 Sept. 2008. Web. Web. 31 Dec. 2016. <http://www.abc.net.au/news/stories/2008/09/08/2358528.htm>.; Ryall. "Kim Jong-Il 'died in 2003', says Japanese professor."

[164] "Saddam's 'Double' Trouble." WND. N.p. 26 March 2003. Web. 31 Dec. 2016. <http://www.wnd.com/2003/03/17941/>.

ago."[165] Hussein's sons, his first wife, and Deputy Prime Minister, Tariq Aziz, may have used three doubles to hide Hussein's death to maintain their positions.[166]

Even if Hussein did not die from cancer in 1999, it is possible he was killed in a U.S. airstrike that hit Baghdad on March 20, 2003.[167] U.S. intelligence was convinced that Hussein and his sons, Qusay and Uday, had been inside the compound when it was hit.[168] One official said that Hussein had been "at least injured," and that medical aid had been urgently summoned to the scene.[169] Eyewitnesses reported seeing Hussein being taken from the rubble on a "gurney, with an oxygen mask over his face."[170] Former U.S. President, George W. Bush, even announced that Hussein had been hit.[171] Share International issued a press release saying Hussein had

---

[165] "Saddam's 'Double' Trouble: Opposition Leader Claims Hussein Died Of Cancer In 1999." Rense.com. N.p. 26 Mar. 2003. Web. 14 Aug. 2019. <http://www.rense.com/general46/doub.htm>.

[166] *Id.*

[167] McWethy. "Saddam Hit? U.S.: Saddam Seen Leaving Baghdad Complex on a Gurney After Strike."

[168] Cornwell, Rupert. "The Saddam Conundrum: Was He Killed in First Raid?" The Independent. N.p. 22 March 2003. Web. 31 Dec. 2016. <http://www.independent.co.uk/news/world/middle-east/the-saddam-conundrum-was-he-killed-in-first-raid-111874.html>.

[169] *Id.*; *see also* McWethy. "Saddam Hit? U.S.: Saddam Seen Leaving Baghdad Complex on a Gurney After Strike."

[170] McWethy. "Saddam Hit? U.S.: Saddam Seen Leaving Baghdad Complex on a Gurney After Strike."

[171] Cienfuegos, "Iraqi Resistance Stiffens Amidst Claims Saddam's Capture was a Hoax,"

died from his injuries two days after the attack.[172]   In July 2003, former Army intelligence officer, John Loftus, said, "[T]he story down here is that we're not even looking for Saddam Hussein because military intelligence [also United States Central Command and Special Operations Command] is so convinced that he was killed on March 20..."[173]

Within hours of the air raid, however, Hussein appeared on Iraqi television, condemning the U.S. attacks and calling on Iraqis to defend their country against its enemies.[174] A major debate flared up among U.S. officials about whether it was really Hussein or not.[175] Many who saw the speech thought it was an impostor.[176] "Hussein" was wearing glasses, which he did not usually do.[177] The bespectacled man looked puffy, old and tired, and did not seem "robust" as Hussein had done just three days earlier.[178] Jerrald Post, the founder of the CIA's Psychological Profile Unit, said his initial reaction was "Gee. That does not look like him."[179]

---

[172] "It's Not Saddam: A Story Calling for Investigation." Share International, N.p. 21 Dec. 2003. Web. 31 Dec. 2016. <http://www.globalresearch.ca/articles/CRG312B.html>.

[173] "Text of Interview with John Loftus." MSNBC. N.p. 25 July 2003. Web. 31 Dec. 2016. <http://www.globalresearch.ca/articles/CRG312B.html>.

[174] McWethy. "Saddam Hit? U.S.: Saddam Seen Leaving Baghdad Complex on a Gurney After Strike."

[175] *Id.*

[176] *Id.*

[177] *Id.*

[178] *Id..*

[179] Morales. "CIA: Man On Tape Is Saddam."

Graham Fuller, former vice chairman of the National Intelligence Council at the CIA, explained that a Hussein impostor may have been used for disinformation and propaganda purposes. Fuller said, "The Iraqi regime would want to reassure the public by giving the impression that Saddam and other people around him were alive."[180]

U.S. officials concluded it was Hussein on T.V. after conducting voice analyses and using computer algorithms to compare the speaker's face to known images of Hussein.[181] CIA officials said it was the real Hussein "without his contacts, without his make-up, and without a good night's sleep."[182] Dr. Buhmann agreed, saying he was "almost certain" that it was the real Hussein.[183]

However, then Press Secretary, Ari Fleischer, pointed out that even though it appeared to be Hussein on the tape, there was no way to know *when* the tape was actually recorded.[184] The tape could have been one of several analysts believed Hussein had pre-recorded for just such an occasion.[185] As one official put it, "It was not broadcast live, it could have been taped two minutes before he aired it, or two

---

[180] "Strike on Iraq: Interview With Graham Fuller." N.p. 20 March 2003. Web. 17 Jan. 2017. <http://transcripts.cnn.com/TRANSCRIPTS/0303/20/se.19.html>.

[181] McWethy.. "Saddam Hit? U.S.: Saddam Seen Leaving Baghdad Complex on a Gurney After Strike."

[182] *Id.*

[183] *Id.*

[184] *Id.*

[185] Cornwell. "The Saddam Conundrum: Was He Killed in First Raid?"

days."[186] Loftus noted that "many of the videotapes that were shown during the war were prerecorded and [in] one of them, for example, Saddam is walking by a building that was blown up on the first day of the war..."[187]

In December 2003, Hussein was captured by American forces and transferred to the American military base in Qatar.[188] Many in the Arab and Muslim world doubted that the real Hussein had been captured.[189] In the Iraqi cities of Fallujah and Mosel, there were protests against the "Saddam capture hoax."[190] A taxi driver named "Diaa" scoffed at the idea that the real Hussein had been caught.[191] He said, "everyone knows that Saddam dyes his hair, but after eight months hiding in a hole, it's still black? Tell me how this is possible..."[192]

---

[186] *Id.*

[187] "Text of Interview with John Loftus."

[188] Pogodin, Maxim. "Saddam's wife could not recognize her husband." Pravda.ru. N.p. 13 April 2004. Web. 31 Dec. 2016. <http://web.archive.org/web/20040606051747/http://english.pravda.ru/world/20/91/366/12494_saddam.html>.

[189] Cienfuegos, "Iraqi Resistance Stiffens Amidst Claims Saddam's Capture was a Hoax."

[190] *Id.*

[191] MacKinnon, Mark. "Iraqis doubt real Hussein behind bars." The Globe and Mail. N.p. 18 Dec. 2003. Web. 31 Dec. 2016. <http://www.theglobeandmail.com/news/world/iraqis-doubt-real-hussein-behind-bars/article1170845/>.

[192] *Id.*

Thousands of Iraqis who had known Hussein claimed that the captive was one of his doubles.[193] Hussein's eldest daughter, Raghad Hussein, said she and her family did not believe the pictures were really of her father.[194] She said, "This is not our father! This is not how he would act."[195]

When Hussein's wife, Sajida Heiralla Tuffah, went to meet with him at the end of March 2004, she exclaimed, "This is not my husband but his double. Where is my husband? Take me to my husband."[196] American officials tried to convince her that Hussein had changed a lot while in custody and that was why she did not recognize him.[197] Tuffah responded furiously, "You think I do not know my husband? I was married to the man for more than twenty-five years!"[198]

---

[193] Cienfuegos, "Iraqi Resistance Stiffens Amidst Claims Saddam's Capture was a Hoax."

[194] *Id.*

[195] *Id.*

[196] Pogodin. "Saddam's wife could not recognize her husband."; Vialls Joe. "Mrs Saddam says Saddam is not Saddam." Propagandamatrix.com. N.p. 18 June 2004. Web. 31 Dec. 2016. <http://www.propagandamatrix.com/articles/june2004/180604saddamnotsaddam.htm>.

[197] *Id.*

[198] *Id.*

Saddam Hussein: 1998 (left)[199] vs. 2003 (right)[200]

Parisoula Lampsos, Hussein's mistress for nearly thirty years, agreed that the prisoner was not the real Saddam Hussein.[201] Lampsos could tell, because Hussein had two dots tattooed on his left hand.[202] In the video that showed a U.S.

---

[199] Photo by Iraqi News Agency - Getty Images, Public Domain, https://commons.wikimedia.org/w/index.php?curid=54584022.

[200] Photo by Unknown - http://www.dodmedia.osd.mil/DVIC_View/Still_Details.cfm?SDAN=DDSD0501884&JPGPath=/Assets/2005/DoD/DD-SD-05-01884.JPG, Public Domain, https://commons.wikimedia.org/w/index.php?curid=99989.

[201] McWethy. "Saddam Hit? U.S.: Saddam Seen Leaving Baghdad Complex on a Gurney After Strike."; McWethy, John and Brian Ross, Pierre Thomas and Martha Raddatz. "U.S. Officials: Saddam Seen on Gurney." ABC News. N.p. 21 March 2003. Web. 31 Dec. 2016. <http://abcnews.go.com/International/story?id=79614&page=1>; Cienfuegos. "Iraqi Resistance Stiffens Amidst Claims Saddam's Capture was a Hoax."

[202] McWethy. "Saddam Hit? U.S.: Saddam Seen Leaving Baghdad Complex on a Gurney After Strike."

Army medic checking his throat, the tattoo was nowhere to be seen.[203] Lampsos felt that the eyes were the real giveaway, though.[204] She said, "You can change your teeth, everywhere. But the eyes, no."[205]

Jassim Abu Ahmed, an athlete who had known Hussein's eldest son Uday personally, said he was certain the bedraggled person the United States paraded around was not the real Hussein and "everybody knows it's not him."[206]

Iraqi claims that the U.S. had captured a Hussein double may have been an effort to demoralize the enemy.[207] On the other hand, "the pictures could be part of a U.S. ploy or Saddam's own strategy to create a double and flee attempts to capture him," according to Abu Haniffa, the president of the Sri Lanka Traders' Association.[208] Waleed Ibrahim of Fallujah asserted that "It is someone wearing a Saddam mask. It is a trick to help President Bush get re-elected."[209]

During the trial, the prisoner acknowledged that he was Saddam Hussein.[210] However, some reporters wondered why

---

[203] MacKinnon. "Iraqis doubt real Hussein behind bars."

[204] McWethy. "Saddam Hit? U.S.: Saddam Seen Leaving Baghdad Complex on a Gurney After Strike."

[205] *Id.*

[206] MacKinnon. "Iraqis doubt real Hussein behind bars."

[207] Pogodin. "Saddam's wife could not recognize her husband."

[208] Cienfuegos. "Iraqi Resistance Stiffens Amidst Claims Saddam's Capture was a Hoax."

[209] MacKinnon. "Iraqis doubt real Hussein behind bars."

[210] Vialls, Joe. "Shaddam Shaddam's New Vaudeville Scam!" Joevialls.altermedia.info. N.p. 3 July 2004. Web. 31 Dec. 2016. <http://web.archive.org/web/20040704142248/http://joevialls.altermedia.info/iraq/vaudeville.html>.

Hussein, who had previously been fastidious about being clean shaven and having neat hair, would suddenly change his habits and appear like a vagabond with long disheveled hair and a bushy, unkempt beard.[211]

Journalists were only shown sketches at trial, because "no photographs of Saddam Hussein [were] allowed due to high security."[212] The only person who was allowed to photograph Hussein in court was CNN's Christiane Amanpour.[213] This trial footage may prove that the prisoner was not Hussein due to some physical anomalies.[214] For example, the real Hussein had an overbite, i.e. his upper teeth closed in front of his lower teeth.[215] The Hussein depicted in at least fifty of Amanpour's video frames had an underbite, i.e. the lower teeth closed in front of the upper teeth.[216] It is possible that the bushy beard was meant to conceal the underbite or the jawline of an impostor.[217] "Shaddam," as the suspected Hussein double was dubbed, also had "highly irregular lower teeth," while Hussein had white, even teeth that were in pristine condition.[218] Hussein's teeth and the

---

[211] *Id.*

[212] *Id.*

[213] Bancroft-Hinchey, Timothy. "This is not Saddam." Pravda.ru. N.p. 7 July 2004, Web. 31 Dec. 2016. <http://web.archive.org/web/20040903014153/http://english.pravda.ru/printed.html?news_id=13298>.

[214] Vialls. "Shaddam Shaddam's New Vaudeville Scam!"

[215] *Id.*

[216] *Id.*

[217] *Id.;* Bancroft-Hinchey. "This is not Saddam."

[218] Bancroft-Hinchey. "This is not Saddam"; Vialls. "Shaddam Shaddam's New Vaudeville Scam!"

prisoner's teeth were "wholly and totally different."[219] Another disparity was that the tip of the nose of the captive was much broader than the real Hussein's.[220]

The video broadcast of "Hussein's" execution on December 30, 2006 showed that there was a mole on the right side of the face where the real Hussein did not have one.[221] Author Anis El-Dighidy studied 7,890 photos of Hussein, including 120 videos of his speeches and interviews, concluded that the real Hussein had not been captured, much less executed, in his aptly entitled book, *Saddam Was Not Executed*.[222]

Similarly to Hussein, Oswald may have been impostor-replaced. Author Robert Cutler claimed in *Alias Oswald* that a Russian-speaking person had taken Oswald's place during his stint in the Marines.[223] It was this Russian-speaking "Oswald" who, while working for the CIA, "defected" to Russia in October 1959 and was later accused of assassinating Kennedy.[224]

Oswald's defection may have been staged, because the CIA and military intelligence tried to plant "defector"

---

[219] Bancroft-Hinchey. "This is not Saddam."

[220] "It's Not Saddam: A Story Calling For Investigation."

[221] El Mallah, "Anis El-Dighidy."

[222] *Id.*

[223] Armstrong. "JFK 101: An excerpt from 'Harvey & Lee: How the CIA Framed Oswald."

[224] *Id.*

operatives inside the USSR during this time frame.[225] A declassified government document proved Oswald was trained by the CIA.[226] It is possible that the Russians used the American deception against them by replacing their Oswald with a "Manchurian Candidate" impostor of their own.[227]

In *Legend of Lee Harvey Oswald*, author Edward Epstein suggested that the Russians substituted a lookalike for the real Oswald during his defection to the USSR.[228] Similarly, Michael Eddowes opined in *The Oswald File* that the Oswald who returned from Russia in 1962 was not the same Oswald who defected in 1959, but instead was a KGB impostor who used the name "Alek Hidell."[229]

After his arrest, Oswald was carrying two Selective Service Registration Cards - one was his own, but one had "Alek Hidell" on it.[230] Oswald denied using the name Alek

[225] Rosenbaum, Ron. "Still on the Case." Texas Monthly. N.p. Nov. 1983. Web. 30 Dec. 2016. p. 270. <http://www.texasmonthly.com/politics/still-on-the-case/>.

[226] Memo from CIA Director, John McCone, dated March 3, 1964. "De-Classified Document Admits Lee Harvey Oswald Was CIA." Federal Jack. Web. 31 Dec. 2016. <http://www.federaljack.com/de-classified-document-admits-lee-harvey-oswald-was-CIA/>.

[227] "Interview with the Assassin: Misinformaton."

[228] Armstrong. "JFK 101: An excerpt from 'Harvey & Lee: How the CIA Framed Oswald.'"

[229] "Pieces of the Puzzle: Great Moments in the Conspiracy Timeline." Texas Monthly. N.p. Nov. 1983. Web. 30 Dec. 2016. p. 156. <http://www.texasmonthly.com/articles/pieces-of-the-puzzle/>.

[230] Marrs, Jim. "[Marrs Jim] Crossfire, The Plot That Killed Kenned (BookZa.org).HTML." Docshare.tips. N.p. June 2016. Web. 30 Dec. 2016. <http://docshare.tips/marrs-jim-crossfire-the-plot-that-killed-kennedbookzaorghtml_576c5fe8b6d87f8a3c8b4953.html?utm_source=docshare&utm_medium=sidebar&utm_campaign=5758c141b6d87fa8218b45c7>.

Hidell or knowing anyone by that name.[231] When confronted, Oswald refused to tell why he was carrying the card or the use he made of it."[232] James Leavelle of the Dallas Police recalled that Oswald "was asked, 'Isn't it true that when you was arrested, you had a picture I.D. on there with A. Hidell on it?' He said, 'I believe that's correct.' And he was asked, 'Well, how do you explain that?' and he says, 'I don't.'"[233] It is possible, then, that Oswald's impostor-replacement was actually set up as the patsy for the Kennedy and Tippit murders.

As has been shown in this chapter, doubles can be used for political deceptions that almost defy belief. Such political intrigue is serious business. One false step could give the game away and result in deadly consequences. The next chapter discusses how doubles are prepared for such a role.

---

[231] "Frontline Transcript: Who Was Lee Harvey Oswald?" PBS. Air Date: 16 Nov. 16, 1993.   Web. 31 Dec. 2016. <http://www.pbs.org/wgbh/frontline/film/oswald/transcript/>.

[232] Brussell, Mae. "The Last Words Of Lee Harvey Oswald." N.p. 28 May 1992. Web. 31 Dec. 2016. <http://www.ratical.org/ratville/JFK/LHO.html>.

[233] "Frontline Transcript: Who Was Lee Harvey Oswald?"

5. <u>Double Standard</u>

He's got plastic heart, plastic teeth and toes,
He's got plastic knees and a perfect plastic nose.
He's got plastic lips that hide his plastic teeth and gums,
And plastic legs that reach up to his plastic bum.
~ Ray Davies ~

In any situation in which a *Doppelgänger* is deployed, he must appear to be the real McCoy. The double must be convincing in his appearance and performance. Doubles must emulate the target's behavior and actions, mannerisms, voice and speech tone as closely as possible.[234] The U.S. Office of Strategic Services' *Manual on Personal Disguises* (1944) instructed intelligence officers to "Know the character... you will have to be inside and out - their clothes, facial expressions, gait, gestures, personal habits, thoughts and reactions."[235]

Former dictator of Panama, Manuel Noriega, had four decoys who "practiced his gait, his manner of speech and his modus operandi – what he did during the day and night,"[236] M. E. Clifton James studied General Montgomery's speech, mannerisms, and other characteristics while assigned to his

---

[234] Wallace, Robert and H. Keith Melton. *Spycraft*. USA: Dutton, 2008. p. 387. Print.

[235] De La Garza, Paul. "The secrets behind the spies." St. Petersburg Times, N.p. 15 Aug. 2002. Web. 31 Dec. 2016. <http://www.sptimes.com/2002/08/15/Floridian/The_secrets_behind_th.shtml>.

[236] According to Joe R. Reeder, a former undersecretary for the U.S. Army. Dean. "Politicians' Body Doubles Nothing New."

staff.[237] James had to quit smoking, because Monty was a non-smoker.[238]

To nail the details, the double may carefully study video and audio recordings made of the target.[239] Dadaev watched movies of Stalin to copy the dictator's movements and intonation.[240] Yahia, who worked as Uday Hussein's double for over four years in the late 1980s and early 1990s, was "made to watch videotapes of Uday, to study how the man walked and talked..."[241]

To perfect their performance, some doubles may receive special training in how to speak and act like their target. Stalin double, "Rashid," studied with Alexei Dikiy, an actor who played the part of Stalin in films.[242] Dadaev, a former actor, spent months in training - some of it under the watchful eye of Stalin's feared chief of secret police, Lavrentiy Beria.[243] Dadaev said his "ability to copy Stalin's manners, voice and walk was far more important" than his looks.[244] "[T]he key thing was to get the step right. When

---

[237] Hill. "The Imposter General: Bernard Montgomery's D-Day Body Double."

[238] *Id.*

[239] "Saddam's 'Double' Trouble."

[240] Stewart. "The man who was Stalin's body double finally tells his story."

[241] Recknagel. "Iraq: Seeing Double In Baghdad -- Saddam Uses Look-Alikes To Disguise His Whereabouts"; Copel. "Body Double: Both Sides Of the Ploy."

[242] "Rashid, Josef Stalin's stand-in."

[243] Stewart. "The man who was Stalin's body double finally tells his story."

[244] *Id.*

Stalin was among his entourage, his walk was prompt and firm..."[245]

Saddam Hussein's doubles were also trained extensively in his mannerisms, the way he walked, even his facial tics.[246] They could mimic Hussein's gestures and expressions perfectly, but they rarely spoke, because Hussein had an inimitable lisp.[247]

For the doubles psy-op to be successful, it is critical that the impostor look like the target as much as possible. An already strong resemblance can be improved with disguises, prosthetics, and plastic surgery. For example, while working for the CIA, Robert Barron used disguises and prosthetics to create convincing doubles.[248]

Disguise specialists can make a double match any photographic documents in existence.[249] They can change hair color, eye color, apply facial hair, modify jaw and mouth lines, improvise dental work, create wrinkles, change the complexion, or add glasses and warts to match the target.[250] Other prostheses include noses, chins, skin, ears, eyes and

---

[245] *Id.*

[246] Morales. "CIA: Man On Tape Is Saddam."; Zeller. "The World; Will the Real Saddam Hussein Please Step Down."; "Austria's Haider Met Saddam Lookalike--Report."

[247] "Austria's Haider Met Saddam Lookalike--Report."; Zeller. "The World; Will the Real Saddam Hussein Please Step Down."

[248] Sloan, Tim. "Ex-CIA Disguise Master Helps Disfigured People." Sawfnews.com. N.p. 11 Dec. 2005. Web. 30 Dec. 2016. <http://web.archive.org/web/20100721123311/http://www.sawfnews.com/lifestyle/4825.aspx>.

[249] Wallace. *Spycraft.* p. 387.

[250] *Id.*

sockets, fingers, nipples, and dental appliances.[251] Even partial or whole face masks of the target can be created.

Disguise specialists helped Dadaev look like the much older Stalin. Dadaev was only in his twenties, but the clever use of make-up and disguises helped him pass as the sixty-year-old Stalin.[252]

Monty's double, James, had lost his middle finger on his right hand during World War I, so a prosthetic replacement finger was fashioned for him.[253]

Shelley claimed that Churchill once complimented him for getting the teeth right, having "taken his own false teeth out for the part."[254]

Prostheses have been around since ancient times, but great improvements have been made by modern surgeons working with medical artists called anaplastologists.[255] For example, silicone, which came into widespread use in the 1970s, looks more realistic than rubber or polyurethane.[256] Silicone can be made to look like real skin by painting

---

[251] A prosthetic nose might be held on by magnets attached to a gold frame. Shipman, Claire. "'Master of Disguise' Changes Many Lives." ABC News. N.p. 29 Nov. 2005. Web. 30 Dec. 2016. <http://abcnews.go.com/Health/Cosmetic/story?id=1354130>; Wallace. *Spycraft*. p. 387; McCombs, Phil. "Crafting Hope." Washington Post. N.p. 12 Jan. 2003. Web. 30 Dec. 2016. <http://www.washingtonpost.com/wp-dyn/content/article/2007/05/22/AR2007052201310_5.html>.

[252] Stewart. "The man who was Stalin's body double finally tells his story."

[253] Hill. "The Imposter General: Bernard Montgomery's D-Day Body Double."

[254] Thorpe. "Finest hour for actor who was Churchill's radio voice."

[255] McCombs. "Crafting Hope."

[256] *Id.*

capillaries, hair follicles, spider veins, and blemishes onto it.[257]

Because one suspicious-looking eyebrow or a misplaced ear could betray an operative and cost him his life, the disguise must be able to pass close inspection at six to twelve inches away.[258] After Barron's stint with the CIA, one of his private clients phoned to complain that his barber had cut off the tiny hairs on his prosthetic ear.[259] Barron "told him to rejoice because even his barber couldn't tell his ear was not real... That's how good the work must be."[260]

In addition to prosthetic body parts, disguise specialists may create doubles by using a silicone face mask.[261] A company called SPFXMasks uses silicone that looks and feels like real skin to create hyper-realistic face masks.[262] The "skin" even has pores.[263] The inside of the mask is smooth, so it stretches over the face and moves with the facial muscles naturally.[264]

The masks are realistic enough that agents can pass

---

[257] Laytner, Ron. "The Man Who Makes Faces." Edit International. N.p. 2009. Web. 30 Dec. 2016. <http://web.archive.org/web/20120201021741/ http://www.editinternational.com/read.php?id=47dddf8c807d1>; Shipman. "'Master of Disguise' Changes Many Lives."; McCombs. "Crafting Hope."

[258] Shipman. "'Master of Disguise' Changes Many Lives."

[259] Laytner. "The Man Who Makes Faces."

[260] *Id.*

[261] Shipman. "'Master of Disguise' Changes Many Lives."

[262] Bernstein, Sharon. "Masks so realistic they're arresting the wrong guy." Los Angeles Times. N.p. 8 Dec. 2010. Web. 30 Dec. 2016. <http:// articles.latimes.com/2010/dec/08/business/la-fi-mask-20101209>.

[263] *Id.*

[264] *Id.*

within a few feet of a border guard in bright sunlight and remain undetected.[265] Hand and arm "gloves" are worn that match the mask so that no suspicious difference in skin tone can be detected.[266]

A face mask can be so effective that it can even change a person's racial or gender appearance.[267] Former chief of disguise at the CIA, Jonna Mendez, was a white woman who once successfully passed herself off as a black man.[268] Likewise, Conrad Zdzierak was a white man who used an SPFX Mask to disguise himself as a black man during a series of Ohio bank robberies.[269] Six of seven bank tellers mistakenly identified an African American man as the culprit.[270] A 20-year-old Chinese man seeking asylum in Canada used one of the SPFX Masks to transform himself into an elderly white man.[271] He was able to slip past airport security in Hong Kong unnoticed.[272]

While makeup and disguise artists are adept at making temporary physical changes in a double, plastic surgery is commonly used for more permanent changes.[273] "[T]urning to

---

[265] McCombs. "Crafting Hope."

[266] Wallace. *Spycraft.* p. 387.

[267] *Id.*

[268] De La Garza. "The secrets behind the spies."

[269] Bernstein. "Masks so realistic they're arresting the wrong guy."

[270] *Id.*

[271] *Id.*

[272] *Id.*

[273] Zeller. "The World; Will the Real Saddam Hussein Please Step Down."

plastic surgery for more permanent alterations is common in every corner of international intrigue."[274]

Plastic surgery can make features more or less prominent.[275] Thin lips can be plumped up with injections, or the external form of the ear or the earlobes can be changed.[276] Other features can even be removed.[277]

The British Special Operations Executive (SOE) used plastic surgery to facilitate espionage and sabotage behind enemy lines during World War II.[278] SOE had a stable of plastic surgeons who could permanently alter agents' faces.[279] For example, one Jewish agent underwent radical surgery to look more German so that he could work as a spy and saboteur in Nazi Germany.[280]

---

[274] *Id.*

[275] Recknagel. "Iraq: Seeing Double In Baghdad -- Saddam Uses Look-Alikes To Disguise His Whereabouts."

[276] *Id.*; Knight, Katherine and Kelly Strange. "The 50-year-old mother who has spent £10,000 on surgery to look like her daughter," Daily Mail Online. N.p. 17 April 2009. Web. 31 Dec. 2016. <http://www.dailymail.co.uk/femail/article-1170348/The-50-year-old-mother-spent-10-000-surgery-look-like-daughter.html#ixzz0wdt9lqFM>.

[277] Recknagel. "Iraq: Seeing Double In Baghdad -- Saddam Uses Look-Alikes To Disguise His Whereabouts."

[278] Ross, Bernie. "Training SOE Saboteurs in World War Two." BBC News. N.P. 17 Feb. 2011. Web. 31 Dec. 2016. <http://www.bbc.co.uk/history/worldwars/wwtwo/soe_training_01.shtml>.

[279] *Id.*

[280] *Id.*

The Germans were also using plastic surgery in the 1940s.[281] A female Nazi intelligence officer named Magda Zeitfeld claimed her father had had the largest plastic surgery clinic in Berlin until his mysterious death in 1943.[282] He had specialized in implanted facial prosthetics, using highly advanced silicates to build up weak jaws and noses.[283]

To become Uday Hussein's double, Yahia "had to have new teeth implanted and plastic surgery done on his chin."[284] He defected, in part, to avoid undergoing yet another painful operation to make him look even more like Uday.[285] Saddam Hussein doubles had to submit to extensive plastic surgery to further improve their resemblance to the former Iraqi leader.[286] One of Kim Jong Il's doubles also had plastic surgery to make his appearance more convincing.[287]

There are limits to what plastic surgery can do, however. It is not possible to correct a badly misshapen jaw

---

281 Kapnistos, Peter Fotis. "Soviet Autopsy: Hitler Died But His Double Escaped." GovernmentSecrets.com. N.p. 2014. Web. 31 Dec. 2016. <http://www.governmentsecrets.com/soviet-autopsy-hitler-died-but-his-double-escaped/#>.

282 *Id.*

283 Kapnistos. "Soviet Autopsy: Hitler Died But His Double Escaped."

284 Copel. "Body Double: Both Sides Of the Ploy."

285 Recknagel. "Iraq: Seeing Double In Baghdad -- Saddam Uses Look-Alikes To Disguise His Whereabouts."

286 *Id.*; Morales. "CIA: Man On Tape Is Saddam."; Zeller. "The World; Will the Real Saddam Hussein Please Step Down."; "Austria's Haider Met Saddam Lookalike--Report."

287 Sheridan. "North Korea 'uses doubles to hide death of Kim.'"

bone or change the length and width of an adult's head.[288] Neither is it possible to surgically alter the tragus (the small piece of cartilage that overhangs the entrance of the ear canal), the nasal spine (the point between the two nostrils where the nose projects out from the face), or the oral commissure (the line formed by the upper lip meeting the lower lip).[289]

Because even slight physical differences can betray a double, distractors may be used.[290] These include a mustache, a beard, a hat, or even unusual clothing.[291] The distractor is used to draw attention to itself, and away from other features. A mustache or a beard has the added advantage of partially obscuring the face. A double might sport a mustache to conceal the nasal spine, a beard to hide the jaw line, or wear his hair long (or a hat) to disguise his head shape.[292] "Shaddam's" bushy beard may have been used to conceal an impostor's jawline or underbite, and his long hair may have been intended to conceal the shape of the skull.[293] In addition, if people notice a difference, they may simply attribute it to new facial hair or a new haircut, and not suspect they are dealing with a double.

---

[288] Vialls. "Shaddam Shaddam's New Vaudeville Scam!"; Recknagel. "Iraq: Seeing Double In Baghdad -- Saddam Uses Look-Alikes To Disguise His Whereabouts."; Di Fabio, Andriola and Alessandra Gigante. "Ask Who Was the 'Beatle.'" Wired Magazine. N.p. 15 July 2009. Web. 31 Dec. 2016. <http://plasticmacca.blogspot.com/2010/01/forensic-science-proves-paul-was.html>.

[289] Di Fabio. "Ask Who Was the 'Beatle.'"

[290] Wallace. *Spycraft.* p. 387.

[291] *Id.*

[292] Vialls. "Shaddam Shaddam's New Vaudeville Scam!"

[293] Bancroft-Hinchey. "This is not Saddam."; Vialls. "Shaddam Shaddam's New Vaudeville Scam!"

The change in Jimmy Carter's appearance and behavior was so noticeable that a distraction was necessary to divert peoples' attention.[294] To that end, the Carter double received "great publicity over the fact that he parts his hair on the left; the old Carter, of course, parted it on the right. So now anyone who looks at him and thinks, 'Carter sure looks different these days,' will also think, 'I guess it's the hair that does it.'"[295]

To step into the target's shoes, the double must make his body conform to the target's build as much as possible. The lookalike may wear padded clothing, which can alter body-shape and weight distribution.[296] If the double were shorter than the target, he could insert shoe lifts to make himself taller.[297] Torso devices can also be used to create a stooped posture,[298]

In some instances, media-manipulation may be used to conceal physical differences in photos and video.[299] For example, if a double is noticeably taller, shorter, heavier or thinner than the target, he may be shown sitting down behind a desk that obscures his torso. If he is shown standing, there may be an absence of reference markers that could reveal his true height. For instance, he would likely not be shown standing next to a person whose height is known, as that could betray a height discrepancy that could out him.

---

[294] Beter. "Audio Letter No. 45."

[295] *Id.*

[296] Wallace. *Spycraft.* p. 387.

[297] *Id.*

[298] *Id.*

[299] *See* Beter. "Audio Letter No. 44."

One can see how much work can go into creating a convincing double. Differences between the target and the impostor can be further camouflaged through the use of technology. This is the topic of the next chapter.

6. <u>Phony Business</u>

We were talking about the... people who hide
themselves behind a wall of illusion.
~ George Harrison ~

Photos, video, and voice can be altered in psy-ops involving doubles.[300] Digital morphing technology can make it appear as though someone said or did something they did not. Photos can be altered to make the double look more like the target, and old pictures of the target can be recycled or modified as part of the subterfuge.

Photo-fakery is nothing new. Photographic alterations have existed almost as long as photography itself (the first permanent photographic image was created in 1826).[301] The Soviet Union was doctoring photos from its earliest days.[302] For example, Soviet censors edited out Nikolai Yezhov from a

---

[300] Arkin, William M. "When Seeing and Hearing Isn't Believing." The Washington Post. N.p. 1 Feb. 1999. Web. 31 Dec. 2016. <http://www.washingtonpost.com/wp-srv/national/dotmil/arkin020199.htm>.

[301] Farid, Hany. "Seeing Is Not Believing." IEEE Spectrum: Technology, Engineering, and Science News. N.p. 31 July 2009. Web. 31 Dec. 2016. <http://spectrum.ieee.org/computing/software/seeing-is-not-believing/0>; "Digital Forensics: Photo Tampering Throughout History [Slide Show]." Scientific American. N.p. 2 June 2008. Web. 31 Dec. 2016. <http://www.scientificamerican.com/slideshow.cfm?id=photo-tampering-throughout-history&%3Bphoto_id=4A94FA96-B59E-3711-A1F5658E0CEC8A7D>.

[302] Cornwell. "The Kim Jong-il that Clinton met was a fake, says academic."

1930s era photo with Stalin after Yezhov was executed in 1940.[303]

Before computers, such fakery required mastery of complicated and time-consuming darkroom techniques.[304] Nowadays, anyone can use powerful and affordable software to doctor digital images to create sophisticated forgeries that can be difficult to detect.[305]

Photos can be stretched, compressed, or blended to improve the likeness of the double to the target or vice versa. If the target has a round, full face, but the double has a longer, thinner face, then photographs of the target could be stretched to make him look more like the double. Likewise, photos of the impostor could be compressed to make the face seem rounder like the target's face.

Composite pictures could also be made by using layers to blend images of the target and the double. For example, the FBI used a photo of Gaspar Llamazares, a Spanish lawmaker, (without his permission) to create an image purporting to be of terrorist extremist, Osama bin Laden.[306] Llamazares' hair and facial wrinkles were used, because "the forensic artist was unable to find suitable features among the reference

---

[303] E., Ryan. "Stalin's Revision of History." Prezi.com. N.p. 3 Jan. 2013. Web. 31 Dec. 2016. <https://prezi.com/3vl7nrhgj9eg/stalins-revision-of-history/>.

[304] Farid. "Seeing Is Not Believing."

[305] *Id.*

[306] Heckle, Harold. "Spanish lawmaker's photo used for bin Laden poster." Newsday. N.p. 16 Jan. 2010. Web. 31 Dec. 2016. <http://www.newsday.com/news/nation/spanish-lawmaker-s-photo-used-for-bin-laden-poster-1.1705738>.

photographs," so he "cut and paste[d] in Photoshop a photograph he found out there on the Internet."[307]

The backyard photograph of Oswald that appeared on the cover of the February 21, 1964 *LIFE* magazine is a suspected forgery. Oswald complained, "That picture is not mine, but the face is mine. The picture has been made by superimposing my face. The other part of the picture is not me at all, and I have never seen this picture before... It was entirely possible that the Police Department has superimposed this part of the photograph over the body of someone else... The small picture was reduced from the larger one... Since I have been photographed at City Hall, with people taking my picture while being transferred from the office to the jail door, someone has been able to get a picture of my face, and with that, they have made this picture..."[308]

Robert Blakey, who served as Chief Counsel to the House Select Committee on Assassinations (HSCA) during its reinvestigation of the death of Kennedy in 1977-78, said that, if the photo had been doctored, it would be evidence of a conspiracy to frame Oswald.[309] Blakey told HSCA, "If [the backyard photographs of Oswald] are invalid, how they were produced poses far-reaching questions in the area of conspiracy, for they evince a degree of technical sophistication that would almost necessarily raise the possibility that

---

[307] *Id.*

[308] Brussell. "The Last Words Of Lee Harvey Oswald."

[309] Fetzer, Jim and Jim Marrs. "JFK Assassination. False Flag Attacks: How 'Patsies' are Framed." Globalresearch.ca. N.p. 11 Dec. 2009. Web. 30 Dec. 2016. <http://www.globalresearch.ca/index.php?context=va&aid=16224>.

[someone] conspired not only to kill the President, but to make Oswald a patsy."[310]

According to North Korea expert, Aidan Foster-Carter, the North Koreans have "faked pictures from way back..."[311] They do not hesitate to tamper with photographs to serve ideological purposes.[312] They would have altered pictures of Kim Jong Il to prove he was alive and well, in charge, and not incapacitated.[313]

Some photographs purportedly of Kim may have been of a double, or were perhaps recycled earlier pictures of him.[314] Korean specialist, Choi Jin-Wook, suspected that North Korean photo editors had been pasting in old pictures of Kim from when he was in good health into photos from trips he supposedly took in 2009.[315] Other analysts believed a look-alike had been standing in for him.[316] Radio host, Ha Tae-kyung, observed, "Most of the pictures put out by North Korean authorities are not the real Kim Jong-Il."[317]

---

[310] *Id.*

[311] "'Fake photo' revives Kim rumours." BBC News. N.p. 12 Nov. 2008. Web. 31 Dec. 2016. <http://news.bbc.co.uk/2/hi/7715458.stm>.

[312] *Id.*

[313] *Id.*

[314] Kirk. "Would the real Kim Jong-Il please sit back down in his wheelchair?"

[315] Kirk. "Did President Clinton meet N. Korea's Kim Jong-il or his look-alike?"

[316] *Id.*

[317] Kirk. "Would the real Kim Jong-Il please sit back down in his wheelchair?"

One image of Kim suspected of being a forgery was released in October 2008.[318] It showed lush foliage in the background that belied the supposed autumn timeframe.[319]

Another photo published by Korean Central News Agency (KCNA) on June 14, 2009 showed Kim wearing a winter jacket during the height of summer.[320]

Pyongyang's state T.V. showed a photo of Kim (also on June 14, 2009) that appeared to be a doctored version of one published on April 25, 2008 by KCNA.[321] This photo, which showed Kim visiting an army unit, was nearly identical to the April picture.[322] The positioning of many of the people in the photos was largely the same, except for a dozen figures who did not appear in the later image.[323] Intelligence officials said there was "a high possibility" the April image was recycled.[324]

Video fakery may also be used to dupe the public in doubles psy-ops. The authenticity of the Saddam Hussein execution video, for example, has been called into question. El-Dighidy contended that he had evidence that American forces simply filmed "Hussein" standing with the noose around his neck, and then yelled out "Cut! That's a wrap!"[325]

---

[318] "'Fake photo' revives Kim rumours."

[319] *Id.*

[320] "Kim Jong Il Photo A Fake, Report Claims." CBS News. N.p. 29 Jan. 2009. Web. 31 Dec. 2016. <http://www.cbsnews.com/stories/2009/06/29/world/main5122022.shtml>.

[321] *Id.*

[322] *Id.*

[323] *Id.*

[324] "Kim Jong Il Photo A Fake, Report Claims."

[325] El Mallah, "Anis El-Dighidy."

His theory was that "When the Americans caught [the Hussein look-alike] in the hole that he was in, they had two options, either to kill him then and there and say that they killed 'Hussein'... or to give him an offer. The offer was that he be given the glory of continuing to be Hussein and go through trial, then a 'fake' execution [after which] he would be let go."[326]

Video editing techniques could also make it seem like someone is answering new questions in an interview, but the person may not be there at all.[327] For example, a previous recording of a public figure could be spliced together with a newer recording of an interviewer posing questions that were designed to fit answers on the earlier recording.[328] A double could be mixed in with the recycled video footage of the target to make the video seem current.[329]

This was supposedly the scenario that occurred on the March 25, 1979 episode of NBC's *Meet the Press* with guest, Henry Kissinger.[330] Dr. Beter explained, "[T]hat was the real Henry Kissinger answering questions;... But... the 'Meet the Press' program of last Sunday... was carefully doctored so that Kissinger appeared to be answering new and up-to-date questions... Kissinger was periodically taping interviews to be kept on hand for instant use whenever they might prove useful. All of Kissinger's answers that you saw and heard last Sunday were taped over two months ago on Saturday, January

---

[326] *Id.*

[327] Beter. "Audio Letter No. 44."

[328] *Id.*

[329] *Id.*

[330] *Id.*

20, 1979... Each of the four panelists asked questions which were designed to fit Kissinger's answers of two months ago. In addition, several scenes were shot using a look-alike to be used at commercial breaks and at the end... Finally, computerized video tape editing techniques were used to splice together the new questions, Kissinger's old answers, and the 'break' scenes."[331]

Psychological warfare operations can also involve assassinating a leader's character. A public figure can be discredited by using a double to make it appear he said or did something he really did not.[332] Barnwell, Hillary Clinton's impersonator, "said she has to act responsibly when performing as Clinton and turns down jobs that she feels are inappropriate or could damage the politician's reputation."[333] In a psy-op, a politician could be discredited on purpose to weaken his political position. For example, videos of a leader's lookalike could be released that make it appear that he was doing something to show weakness (perhaps crying) or was involved in some sexually compromising situation.[334]

A former CIA officer admitted that a video of "Osama bin Laden" and his followers sitting around a campfire "swigging bottles of liquor and savoring their conquests with boys" was made by the CIA using "some of us darker-skinned

---

[331] Beter. "Audio Letter No. 44."

[332] Stein, Jeff. "CIA unit's wacky idea: Depict Saddam as gay." The Washington Post. N.p. 25 May 2010. Web. 31 Dec. 2016. <http://web.archive.org/web/20101118063712/http://blog.washingtonpost.com/spy-talk/2010/05/cia_group_had_wacky_ideas_to_d.html>.

[333] Kitching. "Is this the greatest Hillary lookalike in the world? Advertising executive quit her job to impersonate the presidential candidate full-time."

[334] Arkin. "When Seeing and Hearing Isn't Believing."

employees" as actors.[335] Such behavior would have been frowned upon by bin Laden's followers and could have weakened his support.

During the planning stages prior to the 2003 U.S. invasion of Iraq, the CIA's Iraq Operations Group considered making a video of "Saddam Hussein" having sex with a teenage boy to discredit him and destabilize his power base.[336] "It would look like it was taken by a hidden camera... Very grainy, like it was a secret videotaping of a sex session."[337] The plan was to then "flood Iraq with the videos."[338]

Another idea the Iraq Operations Group had was to interrupt Iraqi television programming with a fake special news bulletin.[339] An actor playing Saddam Hussein would announce that he was stepping down in favor of his son, Uday.[340] "Hussein" would say, "I'm sure you will throw your support behind His Excellency, Uday."[341] The ideas also included inserting fake crawls (messages at the bottom of the T.V. screen) into Iraqi newscasts.[342]

Since then, improvements have been made in technology. Digital morphing was developed as a secret

---

[335] Stein. "CIA unit's wacky idea: Depict Saddam as gay."

[336] *Id.*

[337] *Id.*

[338] *Id.*

[339] *Id.*

[340] *Id.*

[341] *Id.*

[342] *Id.*

weapon for use in psy-ops.[343] This military-based technology includes both voice and video morphing.

Voice morphing was developed at the Los Alamos National Laboratory in New Mexico shortly after Iraq's invasion of Kuwait in 1990.[344] Voice morphing involves the digital reproduction of a specific person's voice.[345] It "is a technique for modifying a source speaker's speech to sound as if it was spoken by some designated target speaker."[346] In other words, it can turn one person's voice into another person's.[347] Heads of state could have their voices impersonated to make it sound as though they said something they did not.

In the past, voice-morphing technology cut and pasted letters or words together to make a composite.[348] According to aviator and film director, Howard Hughes, such technology

---

343 Poole-Robb, Stuart. "How cyber criminals are embracing voice morphing." ITProPortal. N,p. 9 Oct. 2015. Web. 13 Jan. 2017. <http://www.itproportal.com/2015/10/09/how-cyber-criminals-are-embracing-voice-morphing/>.

344Arkin. "When Seeing and Hearing Isn't Believing."; Poole-Robb. "How cyber criminals are embracing voice morphing."

345 Poole-Robb. "How cyber criminals are embracing voice morphing."

346 Sivaraman, K. "Voice Morphing." International Journal of Computer Trends and Technology (IJCTT) – volume 3 Issue 1 Number 3 – Jan 2012. Web. 13. Jan. 2017. <http://www.ijcttjournal.org/Volume3/issue-1/number-3/IJCTT-V3I1N3P3.pdf>.

347 Arkin. "When Seeing and Hearing Isn't Believing."

348 *Id.*

could already mimic someone back in 1972.[349] Hughes said, "It is possible to keep a man's death hidden for several years through use of computerized voice tapes which can continue to communicate and even answer questions completely in character by means of telephone. It is possible even now to select, by use of a computer, words, phrases, even inflections out of a mass of taped sounds in the subject's own voice, so that one would believe he was actually speaking to the person himself... [it is possible that] a man's death could actually be hidden for a number of years to all but a trusted and loyal few."[350]

Early voice-morphing technology could sound robotic, but current technology imitates a person's voice by cloning speech patterns and sounds much more convincing.[351] In earlier versions, scientists needed a ten-minute digital recording of a person's voice to get the full range, which they used to create a facsimile in near real time.[352] Nowadays, it is possible to clone an individual's speech patterns in real-time.[353] All that is needed is a voice sample, which can be obtained via a telephone conversation or a video recording.[354]

Digital morphing of videos, such as Computer Generated Imagery (CGI), is another example of a technology

---

[349] Brussell, Mae and Stephanie Caruana. "Is Howard Hughes Dead and Buried Off a Greek Island?" Playgirl Magazine. N.p. Dec. 1974. Web. 31 Dec. 2016. <http://web.archive.org/web/20090308132034/http://www.newsmakingnews.com/mbhowardhughes.htm>.

[350] *Id.*

[351] Arkin. "When Seeing and Hearing Isn't Believing."

[352] *Id.*

[353] Poole-Robb. "How cyber criminals are embracing voice morphing."

[354] *Id.*

that has application in doubles psy-ops. "For Hollywood, it is special effects. For covert operators in the U.S. military and intelligence agencies, it is a weapon of the future."[355]

Actor Brandon Lee was killed on the set of the 1994 movie, "The Crow," before filming was complete.[356] A body double was used for the remaining scenes.[357] Lee's face was digitally composited onto the double's face using CGI.[358] After the manipulation, it was virtually impossible to tell which scenes were with the real Lee, and which were of the double.[359]

CGI was also used in the 1994 movie, "Forrest Gump," in the scenes in which Tom Hanks shook hands with President Kennedy.[360] The filmmakers used "chroma key, warping, morphing and rotoscoping" techniques to place Hanks into these scenes.[361] Voice doubles and other effects were used to

---

[355] Arkin. "When Seeing and Hearing Isn't Believing."

[356] "Greatest Visual and Special Effects (F/X) - Milestones in Film." AMC Filmsite. Web. 5 Jan. 2017. <http://www.filmsite.org/visualeffects15.html>.

[357] *Id.*

[358] *Id.*

[359] *Id.*

[360] Arkin. "When Seeing and Hearing Isn't Believing."

[361] Kendrakahn. "How CGI technology allowed Forrest Gump to meet John F. Kennedy and John Lennon." Storify.com. Web. 5 Jan. 2017. <https://storify.com/kendrakahn/how-cgi-technology-allowed-forrest-gump-meet-john>.

morph and alter Kennedy's mouth to fit the dialogue.[362] CGI was also used to add people to other scenes in the movie.[363]

An advanced version of CGI video morphing technology can be used to clone and animate the image of anyone, which can then be used for counter-intelligence operations.[364] The video of the interview of Wikileaks founder, Julian Assange, by journalist, John Pilger, filmed on October 30, 2016 is suspected of having been altered.[365] Anomalies in the video, such as unusual changes to Assange's left collar and some strange vocal effects, indicate that the new Face2Face video morphing technology may have been used.[366]

Face2Face technology enables a source actor to manipulate the facial expressions of someone in the target video in real time.[367] Its goal "is to animate the facial expressions of the target video by a source actor and re-render

---

[362] *Id.*

[363] *Id.*

[364] Marino, James F. "The FBI Psychological Operation & The Go Betweens Who Furtively Carry Out The FBI's Psychological Warfare Operations." The Mother of All Black Ops. N.p. 30 Sept. 2011. Web. 5 Jan. 2017. <http://9-11themotherofallblackoperations.blogspot.com/2011/09/fbi-psychological-operation-go-betweens.html>.

[365] "The Secrets of the U.S. Election: Julian Assange Talks to John Pilger." Johnpilger.com. N.p. 5 Nov. 2016. Web. 6 Jan. 2017. <http://johnpilger.com/articles/the-secrets-of-the-us-election-julian-assange-talks-to-john-pilger>.

[366] "5 Reasons Julian Assange Interview with John Pilger is FAKE? #WhereisAssange #ProofOfLife." The Outer Dark. N.p. 3 Dec. 2016. Web. 5 Jan. 2016. <https://www.youtube.com/watch?v=anbn3kFL17k>.

[367] Thies, Justus, et al. "Face2Face Real Time Face Capture and Reenactment of RGB Videos." Graphics.stanford.edu. N.p. June 2016. Web. 5 Jan. 2017. <http://www.graphics.stanford.edu/~niessner/thies2016face.html>.

the manipulated output video in a photo-realistic fashion."[368] The software "convincingly re-render[s] the synthesized target face on top of the corresponding video stream such that it seamlessly blends with the real-world illumination."[369]

With the "highly-convincing transfer of facial expressions from a source to a target video in real time" and using virtual dubbing, "it could appear that the target person in the video says something he or she did not say."[370]

Because "it is virtually impossible to notice the manipulations," Face2Face technology has obvious application in psychological warfare operations.[371] Anyone could be made to say anything on a video, and no one would be able to tell the difference.

Samsung has now developed artificial intelligence (AI) software that can generate deepfakes, which are "fabricated clips that make people appear to do or say things they never did," with just one image.[372] Such programs use machine learning to create a video forgery of a moving, speaking

---

[368] *Id.*

[369] *Id.*

[370] *Id.;* "Face2Face: live video editing of facial expressions." Visage Technologies. N.p. 21 March 2016. Web. 9 Jan. 2017. <http://visagetechnologies.com/face2face-live-video-editing-of-facial-expressions/>.

[371] Thies. "Face2Face Real Time Face Capture and Reenactment of RGB Videos."

[372] Solsman, Joan E. "Samsung deepfake AI could fabricate a video of you from a single profile pic. Even the Mona Lisa can be faked." CNet. N.p. 24 May 2019. Web. 14 Aug. 2019. <https://www.cnet.com/news/samsung-ai-deepfake-can-fabricate-a-video-of-you-from-a-single-photo-mona-lisa-cheapfake-dumbfake/?fbclid=IwAR0V7szeAaTFvAIme18FBplbWXT9Cvv-KTUU06NxMI0cdHU8LktNwj7kJBk>.

person, dubbed "realistic neural talking heads."[373] Deepfake technology can be used to place an unsuspecting person's face into a video of another person.[374] The technology can be used for "misinformation, election tampering and fraud, according to Hany Farid, a Dartmouth researcher who specializes in media forensics..."[375]

Sophisticated deepfakes may make mass deception hard to spot. Farid warned, "These results are another step in the evolution of techniques... leading to the creation of multimedia content that will eventually be indistinguishable from the real thing."[376] However, such a forgery may be identified by the fact that the program may miss the finer details, such as failing to reproduce Marilyn Monroe's iconic mole.[377]

This chapter has discussed how technology can be used to deceive people in psy-ops using doubles. The next chapter talks about how technology can be used to uncloak doubles.

---

[373] *Id.*

[374] *Id.*

[375] *Id.*

[376] *Id.*

[377] *Id.*

7. <u>Spot the Impostor</u>

Got nowhere to run to, Baby, nowhere to hide.
~ Brian Holland, et al. ~

Because of the deliberate subterfuge inherent in psy-ops, detecting a double can be difficult. However, comparing both physical and non-physical traits could be revealing. Distinctive physiological and behavioral characteristics are a way to differentiate between lookalikes. For example, one of Kim Jong Il's doubles was exposed in the spring of 2006, when American spy satellite photographs revealed him to be 2.5 cm taller than the real Kim.[378]

Physical features unique to each individual include ears, voice, teeth, dental work, skull shape, and the curves of the eye socket, nose and chin.[379] These are also considered to be immutable characteristics that do not change over time.[380] Photographs, finger- and voiceprints capture these unique identifiers, and may be used to establish identity, and by the

[378] Kuchikomi. "N Korea's Kim Died in 2003; Replaced by Lookalike, Says Waseda Professor."

[379] Vialls. "Shaddam Shaddam's New Vaudeville Scam!"; Bonsor, Kevin and Ryan Johnson. "How Facial Recognition Systems Work." HowStuffWorks.com. N.p. 4 Sept. 2001. Web. 4 Jan. 2017. <http://electronics.howstuffworks.com/gadgets/high-tech-gadgets/facial-recognition2.htm>.

[380] *Pierce v. Dep't of the United States Air Force*, 512 F.3d 184, 188 (5th Cir. Miss. 2007); Bonsor. "How Facial Recognition Systems Work."

same token, determine that an impostor is not who he claims to be.[381]

Photographs of Oswald, the possible victim of impostor-replacement, reveal differences in facial features.[382] In some photos, he appeared to be "scrawny with narrow features," while in others, he seemed to be "thickset and broad."[383] In a photo from the November 1, 1959 issue of *The Fort Worth Star-Telegram*, Oswald looked like a football player, with a large, "bull neck," and a "large, wide nose."[384] Pictures of Oswald in Minsk, Russia depicted a man with a "thicker face, thicker hair, and a broader chin" than the "small, thin, frail-looking man" who was arrested for assassinating Kennedy.[385]

Discrepancies in Oswald's official records also point to a double. On his U.S. Marine Corps records and on his autopsy report, Oswald's height fluctuated from 5'8" in 1956, to 5'11" in 1959, to 5'9" in 1963.[386] Oswald appears to be only slightly taller than his 5'3" wife, Marina, in one picture that shows him standing next to her.[387] After Oswald's arrest, he claimed that he had no permanent scars, but Marine records

---

[381] 5 USCS § 552a(4); *Pierce v. Dep't of the United States Air Force*, 512 F. 3d 184, 188 (5th Cir. Miss. 2007).

[382] Armstrong. "JFK 101: An excerpt from 'Harvey & Lee: How the CIA Framed Oswald.'"

[383] *Id.*

[384] *Id.*

[385] Hildebrand. "The Mystery of Lee Harvey Oswald,"; Armstrong. "JFK 101: An excerpt from 'Harvey & Lee: How the CIA Framed Oswald.'"

[386] *Id.*; Oswald was questioned by Police Officer John Adamcik and FBI Agent M. Clements. Brussell. "The Last Words Of Lee Harvey Oswald."

[387] Hildebrand. "The Mystery of Lee Harvey Oswald."

indicated that he had mastoidectomy scars and scars on his left upper-arm.[388]

A photograph alleged to be of Oswald in Mexico City on October 9, 1963 has been questioned, because the description in CIA cables did not contain accurate descriptions.[389] CIA cable 177 was inaccurate, because Oswald was not as old as described.[390] In addition, he did not have an athletic build, was not six feet tall, and did not have a receding hairline.[391] The description of Oswald in CIA cable 179 was incorrect, because Oswald did not weigh 165 pounds.[392] "Many conspiracy theorists believe that Oswald himself never went to the Cuban and Soviet embassies in Mexico City and that an impersonator, suspected of being CIA agent David Phillips..., was the real visitor to the embassies."[393]

Hussein's doubles were detected by variations in the size of the ears and hands, and shape of the shoulders.[394]

---

[388] *Citing* "Warren Report." pp. 614-618. Brussell. "The Last Words Of Lee Harvey Oswald."

[389] "Scelso," John. "HSCA Security Classified Testimony: 1-37." 16 May 1978. Web. 30 Dec. 2016. <http://www.history-matters.com/archive/jfk/hsca/secclass/Scelso_5-16-78/html/Scelso_0041a.htm>.

[390] "Scelso," John. "HSCA Security Classified Testimony: I-37." Historymatters.com. N.p. 16 May 1978. Web. 4 Jan. 2017. <http://www.history-matters.com/archive/jfk/hsca/secclass/Scelso_5-16-78/html/Scelso_0041a.htm>.

[391] *Id.*

[392] "Scelso," John. "HSCA Security Classified Testimony: 1-44." 16 May 1978. Web. 30 Dec. 2016. <http://www.history-matters.com/archive/jfk/hsca/secclass/Scelso_5-16-78/html/Scelso_0048a.htm>.

[393] "Interview with the Assassin: Misinformaton."

[394] "Austria's Haider Met Saddam Lookalike--Report."

Hussein had wide, strong shoulders, while those of two doubles were narrow and sloping.[395] Hussein had big hands, while one of doubles had small hands.[396] One of the double's index fingers did not match that of the real Hussein.[397] Hussein had an overbite, while one of his doubles did not.[398] John Loftus noted that "This one body double, the chubby one, he's three inches shorter than Saddam and about 30 pounds heavier."[399] Some differences were more subtle, such as the face being just a hair too wide, or the area under the mouth was just a bit too small and too low.[400]

While some physical differences may be detectable with the naked eye, a formal biometrical analysis may sometimes be required to identify a lookalike. The first step is to find suitable images.[401] Next, some markers are laid down for measurements.[402] For example, the distance between the pupils could be set as a baseline for determining the proportions of the target.[403] Computer software can be used to locate specific points on the face.[404] A faceprint can be created

---

[395] "Saddam's 'Double' Trouble."

[396] *Id.*

[397] *Id.*

[398] *Id.*

[399] "Text of Interview with John Loftus."

[400] Zeller. "The World; Will the Real Saddam Hussein Please Step Down."

[401] Di Fabio. "Ask Who Was the 'Beatle.'"

[402] *Id.*

[403] *Id.*

[404] Morales. "CIA: Man On Tape Is Saddam."

using these measurements to compare to photographs.[405] If the measurements do not match on the comparisons, then one is dealing with an impostor.

In 2003, Dr. Buhmann identified three different Hussein's doubles[406] that were used between 1988 and 2002.[407] He examined hundreds of photos and videotapes, comparing pairs of pictures in which Hussein's pose was essentially the same.[408] There were discrepancies in the position of Hussein's facial features and blemishes in various public appearances.[409]

Dr. Buhmann's analysis was based on sophisticated measuring techniques. Using a computer graphics program, he marked each picture to highlight features such as the length and width of the head, the size of the eyelids and nostrils, the shape of the ears and chin, and Hussein's mustache and eyebrow measurements.[410] Computer software located specific points on the face, such as the tip of his nose and the cheekbone, and created a faceprint, which was compared to

---

[405] *Id.*

[406] McWethy. "Saddam Hit? U.S.: Saddam Seen Leaving Baghdad Complex on a Gurney After Strike."

[407] Recknagel. "Iraq: Seeing Double In Baghdad -- Saddam Uses Look-Alikes To Disguise His Whereabouts."; Cienfuegos, "Iraqi Resistance Stiffens Amidst Claims Saddam's Capture was a Hoax."; Morales. "CIA: Man On Tape Is Saddam."

[408] Cienfuegos. "Iraqi Resistance Stiffens Amidst Claims Saddam's Capture was a Hoax,"; Morales. "CIA: Man On Tape Is Saddam."

[409] "Austria's Haider Met Saddam Lookalike--Report."

[410] Cienfuegos. "Iraqi Resistance Stiffens Amidst Claims Saddam's Capture was a Hoax."; Morales. "CIA: Man On Tape Is Saddam."

known photographs of the real Hussein.[411] By overlaying the two pictures, Dr. Buhmann calculated how closely the features matched, indicating whether the person in the pictures was the real Hussein or not.[412] The three Hussein lookalikes all had small, distinct differences.[413]

Facial recognition software is another tool for detecting a double. "Facial recognition is a biometric that uses a unique, measurable characteristic of a person's face for identification."[414] Software automatically compares faces in its image database.[415] Global and fully neural face recognition eliminates identification problems caused by glasses, beards, hairstyles, or even aging.[416] If two pictures of supposedly the same individual do not match, then one is an impostor.

FaceIt® is a facial recognition program that measures the distance between the eyes, the width of the nose, the depth of the eye sockets, the shape of the cheekbones, and the length of the jaw line.[417] These measurements are used to create a

---

[411] Morales. "CIA: Man On Tape Is Saddam."

[412] Cienfuegos. "Iraqi Resistance Stiffens Amidst Claims Saddam's Capture was a Hoax."

[413] Morales. "CIA: Man On Tape Is Saddam."

[414] "What is Facial Recognition?" Facefirst.com. Web. 4 Jan. 2017. <ttp://www.facefirst.com/how-it-works>.

[415] "Phantomas Elaborate Face Recognition." Global-security-solutions.com. Web. 4 Jan. 2017. <http://web.archive.org/web/20090329102843/http://www.global-security-solutions.com/FaceRecognition.htm>.

[416] "Phantomas Elaborate Face Recognition." Global-security-solutions.com. Web. 4 Jan. 2017. <http://web.archive.org/web/20090329102843/http://www.global-security-solutions.com/FaceRecognition.htm>.

[417] Bonsor. "How Facial Recognition Systems Work."

faceprint.[418] FaceIt® is relatively insensitive to changes in expression, and can compensate for facial hair and eyeglasses.[419] The image of a person may be matched to an image in the database to verify that he is who he says he is.[420]

The FaceFirst software algorithm locates the position and size of the face, and the centers of the eyes.[421] Distinguishing features, such as the length of the nose and width of the mouth, are extracted to create a faceprint.[422] Such software could be used to compare the image of the target to that of the suspected double to determine if it is the same person or just a lookalike.

FaceIt®Argus uses skin biometrics to identify individuals.[423] It can even distinguish between identical twins, which is not yet possible using facial recognition software alone.[424] In a process called Surface Texture Analysis, a picture of a patch of skin, called a skin print, is analyzed using computer algorithms.[425] The software documents the skin texture, pores, and any lines in the skin.[426] Skin prints are compared to see if two samples are of the same person or not.

---

[418] *Id.*

[419] *Id.*

[420] *Id.*

[421] "Our Process." Facefirst.com. Web. 4 Jan. 2017. <http:// www.facefirst.com/how-it-works/our-process>.

[422] *Id.*

[423] Bonsor. "How Facial Recognition Systems Work."

[424] *Id.*

[425] *Id.*

[426] *Id.*

Another way to identify a double is to use ear biometrics, as each person's ear has unique characteristics that are different for everyone.[427] Even the ears of identical twins are different.[428] In Germany, there is a craniometrical recognition procedure that uses the right ear for identification purposes that is considered to be equivalent to fingerprints.[429] "Identification by ear biometrics is promising, because it is passive like face recognition... When employing face or lip as a biometric, changing of their appearance with the expression of the subject creates problem[s] but in case of ear the shape and appearance is fixed."[430]

The ears, then, can give away a double. Felix Dadaev admitted as much when he said that he was a perfect Stalin double except for the ears.[431] The CIA was able to determine that Mao Zedong employed a double by studying the impostor's ears.[432] Hussein's doubles were also identified by subtle differences in the size of the ears.[433] Iranian scholar, Mohamed Ismail, who spent twenty-five years studying Hussein's ears, concluded that the ears started to change in

---

[427] Rahman, Md. Mahbubur, et al. "Person Identification Using Ear Biometrics." International Journal of the Computer, the Internet and Management, Vol. 15#2 (May-Aug. 2007), pp. 1-8. Web. 4 Jan. 2017. <http://www.journal.au.edu/ijcim/2007/may07/IJCIMvol15no2_article1.pdf>.; Di Fabio. "Ask Who Was the 'Beatle.'"

[428] Rahman. "Person Identification Using Ear Biometrics."

[429] Di Fabio. "Ask Who Was the 'Beatle.'"

[430] Rahman. "Person Identification Using Ear Biometrics."

[431] Stewart. "The man who was Stalin's body double finally tells his story."

[432] Copel. "Body Double: Both Sides Of the Ploy."

[433] "Austria's Haider Met Saddam Lookalike--Report."

1989.[434] Hussein had big, oval ears that one of the doubles' ears did not match, because of the "special bend."[435]

In the absence of discernible physical differences, one might turn to non-physical criteria to identify a double. Such an analysis might involve implementing behavioral biometrics (a.k.a. behaviometrics). "It's nearly impossible to copy or imitate somebody else's behavior well enough to fool behavioral biometrics verification..."[436] Behaviors, such as gait, voice, or other mannerisms, may expose a *Doppelgänger*.[437]

Analyzing a person's "gait can be used to identify people...; gait is hard to disguise because a person's build and muscles essentially limit their variation of motion..."[438]

A person's voice is considered to be behavioral, because it is based on how a person speaks, such as movement, manner, and pronunciation.[439] Doubles are trained to speak like their target. They mimic the accent and intonation. "The voice is easy to simulate and doubles constantly study video and audio records."[440]

---

[434] El Mallah, "Anis El-Dighidy."

[435] "Saddam's 'Double' Trouble."

[436] Cobb, Michael. "The enterprise potential of behavioral biometrics." Searchsecurity.techtarget.com. Web. 3 Jan. 2017, <http://searchsecurity.techtarget.com/tip/The-enterprise-potential-of-behavioral-biometrics>.

[437] *Id.*

[438] *Id.*

[439] "Voice Verification." Globalsecurity.org. Web. 4 Jan. 2017. <http://www.globalsecurity.org/security/systems/biometrics-voice.htm>.

[440] "Saddam's 'Double' Trouble."

However, voice is also considered to be a physiological trait, because every person has a unique voice print that can be used to establish identity (and detect a double).[441] "The physical shape of the vocal tract is the primary physiological component. The vocal tract is made up [of] the oral and nasal air passages that work with the movement of the mouth, jaw, tongue, pharynx and larynx to articulate and control speech production. 'The physical characteristics of these airways impart measurable acoustic patterns on the speech...'"[442] Voice biometrics technology converts speech to digital format and then extracts "distinctive vocal characteristics, such as pitch, cadence, and tone," to create a voiceprint.[443] Each word is reduced to segments composed of several dominant frequencies called "formants."[444] Each segment has several tones that can be captured in a digital format.[445] The tones collectively identify the speaker's unique voice print.[446]

The combination of the unique physiology and behavioral aspects of the voice enable verification of the identity of the speaker.[447] Voice verification technology uses

---

[441] 5 USCS § 552a(4). *See also United States v. Hawes*, 523 F.3d 245, 249 (3d Cir. Pa. 2008); *United States v. Mitchell*, 518 F.3d 230 (4th Cir. S.C. 2008); *Pierce v. Dep't of the United States Air Force*, 512 F.3d 184, 188 (5th Cir. Miss. 2007).

[442] "Voice Verification."

[443] *Id.*

[444] *Id.*

[445] *Id.*

[446] *Id.*

[447] *Id.*

the unique characteristics of a person's voice to distinguish between different speakers.[448] Different voice prints for supposedly the same person would indicate that one is an impostor.[449]

Voice prints identified a Kim Jong Il double when a Japanese T.V. station compared Kim's voice print from a 2004 meeting with Junichiro Koizumi, the former Japanese prime minister, to an authenticated recording from four years earlier.[450] The voice prints did not match.[451]

Some government officials knew that there was a possibility that heads of state had been meeting with a Kim lookalike. A Japanese official admitted, "Rumors of a dummy Kim began circulating after the [Koizumi 2004] summit. Some of us said we should have Kim's voice prints analyzed. But if we did that and proved the prime minister had been conferring with a double, it could have destroyed the Koizumi administration. So we didn't proceed."[452]

A difference in personality is another non-physical criterion that could reveal a double. According to El-Dighidy, the "Saddam Hussein" who was captured by U.S. forces in 2003 did not behave as the real Hussein would have done. He explained, "The person they caught was not Hussein. There's no way a former dictator and president of a country would allow himself to be mocked the way he was the day he was

---

[448] *Id.*

[449] 5 USCS § 552a(4).

[450] Sheridan. "North Korea 'uses doubles to hide death of Kim.'"

[451] Barlow. "Kim Jong-Il 'died in 2003.'"

[452] Kuchikomi. "N Korea's Kim Died in 2003; Replaced by Lookalike, Says Waseda Professor."

caught. The Hussein that was caught was like a mouse; he was scared, and didn't even try to defend himself."[453]

Some also noted that "Hussein's" body language was different from that of the real Hussein.[454] Falih Abdul Jabbar, a sociologist at London University in England, said the Iraqi public could identify Hussein doubles based on different camera behavior. Jabbar said, "Saddam was very well-known among the Iraqis to be a camera-monger. He loved the camera and to be in close-up shots. And they notice that when the other guy, his 'spare part,' was his replacement, the cameras would take faraway shots, rather than zoom in. They would then deduce this was not the real Saddam."[455]

The Iraqi public could also spot a Hussein double by the behavior of the bodyguards.[456] Jabbar explained, "People noticed that when the other guy, or 'the second Saddam,' was there, they could detect this very easily by looking at the bodyguards, who seemed careless, sometimes even laughing. They wouldn't do that in the presence of the real Saddam."[457]

Discrepancies in Oswald's personality and Russian language ability point to a double, and have even led to speculation that there were two Oswalds involved in some sort

---

[453] El Mallah, "Anis El-Dighidy."

[454] "It's Not Saddam: A Story Calling for Investigation."

[455] Cienfuegos. "Iraqi Resistance Stiffens Amidst Claims Saddam's Capture was a Hoax."

[456] *Id.*; Recknagel. "Iraq: Seeing Double In Baghdad -- Saddam Uses Look-Alikes To Disguise His Whereabouts."

[457] Cienfuegos. "Iraqi Resistance Stiffens Amidst Claims Saddam's Capture was a Hoax."; Recknagel. "Iraq: Seeing Double In Baghdad -- Saddam Uses Look-Alikes To Disguise His Whereabouts."

of an intelligence operation.[458] The people who knew Oswald in New Orleans remembered him differently from those who knew him in Japan.

The Warren Commission's final report put Oswald in the Marine Corps in Atsugi, Japan from September 1957 through May 1958.[459] However, according to Palmer E. McBride's testimony and Marine Corps records, Oswald was in New Orleans at the same time, namely from October 1957 through May 1958.[460]

The Marines in Japan recalled that Oswald was a regular guy from Texas who got drunk on occasion, liked Japanese women, got into fights, and occasionally talked about his family, but never about politics.[461] On the other hand, Oswald in New Orleans frequently discussed communism, did not drink, never talked about his family or background, never got into fights, and threatened to kill President Eisenhower, while the Oswald in Japan never made such a threat.[462]

Beginning in December 1958, Oswald was stationed at the Marine Corps Air Facility in Santa Ana, California, where he constantly discussed politics, favored communism, supported Castro, and suddenly and inexplicably spoke fluent Russian, read Russian literature and newspapers, listened to

---

[458] Armstrong, "JFK 101: An excerpt from 'Harvey & Lee: How the CIA Framed Oswald.'"

[459] *Id.*

[460] *Id.*

[461] *Id.*

[462] *Id.*; Brussell. "The Last Words Of Lee Harvey Oswald."

Russian records, and was interested in everything Russian.[463] During interrogation after his arrest, Oswald said, "I speak Russian, correspond with people in Russia, and receive newspapers from Russia..."[464] According to Warren Commission testimony by people who knew Oswald in Dallas in 1962 and 1963, his command of Russian was exceptional.[465] One witness said that Oswald actually preferred speaking Russian, and could discuss classical Russian literature in Russian.[466]

The Marines in Japan said Oswald had never spoken Russian, never read Russian books, and never listened to Russian records.[467] Marine Zack Stout, stationed with Oswald in Japan, said, "I know Oswald didn't attend any Russian classes or read any Russian books or listen to any Russian records. He didn't have anywhere to get such materials and if he had them we would have known about it... The idea that Oswald studied Russian in Japan is ridiculous - it just didn't happen."[468]

Oswald apparently taught himself to speak Russian well enough to pass a military language exam in a matter of months.[469] However, no one, not even the Warren

------

[463] Armstrong. "JFK 101: An excerpt from 'Harvey & Lee: How the CIA Framed Oswald.'"

[464] Brussell. "The Last Words Of Lee Harvey Oswald."

[465] Armstrong. "JFK 101: An excerpt from 'Harvey & Lee: How the CIA Framed Oswald.'"

[466] *Id.*

[467] *Id.*

[468] *Id.*

[469] *Id.*

Commission, could determine how or where he learned Russian.[470] Oswald could not have taken Russian classes in boot camp (1956), Infantry Training Regiment training at Camp Pendleton (early 1957), aviation training in Jacksonville, Florida (March-April 1957), or radar school in Biloxi, Mississippi (May-June 1957).[471] Different personality traits, Oswald's sudden and near perfect command of the Russian language, and bilocation point to an Oswald double.

Should physical and behavioral methods for detecting a lookalike fail, it may be possible to employ more exotic technology. If a person's unique energy signature or pattern can be identified, then the suspected double's energy pattern could be compared to it. A difference in the energy patterns may be a clue that one is an impostor.

Kirlian photography, which captures a band of light surrounding a person, may be one way. "Variations in the shapes, colors, and intensity of the images produced [by Kirlian photography] are said to provide clues to the patient's overall health and energy level and to indicate the presence or absence of disease, specific emotional states, and other physiological or psychological conditions..."[472] It might be possible to capture the energy pattern surrounding the physical body of the suspected double using Kirlian photography, and compare it to the target's energy pattern.

Another possibility might be to use a device that measures the electronic frequency of a person's energy. The Drown Radio-Vision Instrument, invented in 1935 by Dr. Ruth

---

[470] *Id.*

[471] *Id.*

[472] "Kirlian Photography." Altmd.com. Web. 31 Dec. 2016. <http://www.altmd.com/Articles/Kirlian-Photography--Encyclopedia-of-Alternative-M>.

B. Drown, measures the energy frequency or rates of vibration of matter.[473] "[T]he theory is based on the fact that everything having form in the physical world is made up of molecules... Differing molecular arrangements... produce differing frequencies or vibrations... [I]t has been established firmly that a blood crystal from a human being... carries the complete energy pattern of the owner's body.."[474]

Since a person's blood, at least, holds the unique energy pattern of that individual, this may be a promising method for identifying suspected impostors. If the target's energy pattern can be identified (in a non-invasive way), the suspected double's energy pattern could be compared to it. The energy patterns of the same individual should match. If there is a difference, then that would indicate that one is a *Doppelgänger*.

Several promising new methods for detecting doubles have been discussed in this chapter. Used in combination with historically proven methods, there may soon be no way for doubles to hide. Use every means of identification at your disposal to spot the impostor. Happy hunting!

---

[473] "Radio-Vision: Scientific Milestone." Drown Laboratories. N.p. 1960. Web. 31 Dec. 2016. <http://educate-yourself.org/tjc/radiovisionbookintro30jul03.shtml>.

[474] *Id.*

8. <u>Conclusion</u>

You don't look different, but you have changed
I'm looking through you, you're not the same.
~ Lennon/McCartney ~

While doubles may seem very rare, their use is actually quite widespread in intelligence and politics ("politricks"). Doubles have been employed in psychological warfare operations for centuries. This book has exposed some of the more common uses for them.

There have been a number of body doubles in the past one hundred years. Mata Hari, Joseph Stalin, General Bernard Montgomery, Saddam Hussein, Winston Churchill, and Kim Jong Il are some of the better known examples of historical figures who used doubles to serve a political purpose. Some used doubles in psy-ops to spread disinformation or to enhance security. Others were replaced by impostors to serve as puppets for those who pulled the strings.

Once the reality of the existence of doubles is accepted, recognizing impostors becomes much easier, because the veil of disbelief is lifted. The public is becoming more aware of tactics involved in doubles psy-ops, including the technologies that assist in concealing them. In the future, it will be much more difficult to manipulate people using doubles and impostor-replacements to serve political agendas. The secret is out. Please do not be duped by a double!

Works Cited

5 USCS § 552a(4).

Arkin, William M. "When Seeing and Hearing Isn't Believing." The Washington Post. N.p. 1 Feb. 1999. Web. 31 Dec. 2016. <http://www.washingtonpost.com/wp-srv/national/dotmil/arkin020199.htm>.

Armstrong, John. "Harvey, Lee and Tippit: A New Look at the Tippit Shooting." Kennedys and King. N.p. 15 Feb. 1998. Web. 9 Jan. 2017. <https://kennedysandking.com/john-f-kennedy-articles/harvey-lee-and-tippit-a-new-look-at-the-tippit-shooting>.

Armstrong, John. "JFK 101: An excerpt from 'Harvey & Lee: How the CIA Framed Oswald.'" Web. 30 Dec. 2016. <http://web.archive.org/web/20110404121334/http://www.jfkresearch.com/jfk_101.html>.

"Austria's Haider Met Saddam Lookalike--Report." Reuters, N.p. 6 Oct. 2002, Web. 31 Dec. 2016. <http://web.archive.org/web/20110713071007/http://news1.iwon.com/odd/article/id/272230%7Coddlyenough%7C10-06-2002::12:01%7Creuters.html>.

Bancroft-Hinchey, Timothy. "This is not Saddam." Pravda.ru. N.p. 7 July 2004, Web. 31 Dec. 2016. <http://web.archive.org/web/20040903014153/http://english.pravda.ru/printed.html?news_id=13298>.

Barlow, Karen. "Kim Jong-Il 'died in 2003.'" ABC News. N.p. 7 Sept. 2008. Web. Web. 31 Dec. 2016. <http://www.abc.net.au/news/stories/2008/09/08/2358528.htm>.

Bernstein, Sharon. "Masks so realistic they're arresting the wrong guy." Los Angeles Times. N.p. 8 Dec. 2010. Web. 30 Dec. 2016. <http://articles.latimes.com/2010/dec/08/business/la-fi-mask-20101209>.

Beter, Dr. Peter David. "Audio Letter No. 33." N.p. 28 April 1978. Web. 30 Dec. 2016. <http://www.peterdavidbeter.com/docs/all/dbal33.html>.

Beter, Dr. Peter David. "Audio Letter No. 44." N.p. 29 March 1979. Web. 30 Dec. 2016. <http://www.peterdavidbeter.com/docs/all/dbal44.html>.

Beter, Dr. Peter David. "Audio Letter No. 45." N.p. 27 April 1979. Web. 6 Jan. 2017. <http://www.peterdavidbeter.com/docs/all/dbal45.html>.

Beter, Dr. Peter David. "Audio Letter No. 46." N.p. 28 May 1979. Web. 30 Dec. 2016. <http://www.peterdavidbeter.com/docs/all/dbal46.html>.

"Bolshevik." Encyclopedia Britannica. Web. 17 Jan. 2017. <https://www.britannica.com/topic/Bolshevik>.

Bonsor, Kevin and Ryan Johnson. "How Facial Recognition Systems Work." HowStuffWorks.com. N.p. 4 Sept. 2001. Web. 4 Jan. 2017. <http://electronics.howstuffworks.com/gadgets/high-tech-gadgets/facial-recognition2.htm>.

Branigan, Tania. "Kim Jong-il 'Has Pancreatic Cancer.'" The Guardian UK. N.p. 13 July 2009. Web. 31 Dec. 2016. <https://www.theguardian.com/world/2009/jul/13/kim-jong-il-cancer>.

Brussell, Mae and Stephanie Caruana, "Is Howard Hughes Dead and Buried Off a Greek Island?" Playgirl Magazine. N.p. Dec. 1974. Web. 31 Dec. 2016. <http://web.archive.org/web/20090308132034/http://www.newsmakingnews.com/mbhowardhughes.htm>.

Brussell, Mae. "The Last Words Of Lee Harvey Oswald." N.p. 28 May 1992. Web. 31 Dec. 2016. <http://www.ratical.org/ratville/JFK/LHO.html>.

Cienfuegos, Ernesto. "Iraqi Resistance Stiffens Amidst Claims Saddam's Capture was a Hoax." La Voz de Aztlan. N.p. 16 Dec. 2003. Web. 31 Dec. 2016. <http://web.archive.org/web/20031221100907/http://www.aztlan.net/saddamcapturehoax.htm>.

Cobb, Michael. "The enterprise potential of behavioral biometrics." Searchsecurity.techtarget.com. Web. 3 Jan. 2017, <http://searchsecurity.techtarget.com/tip/The-enterprise-potential-of-behavioral-biometrics>.

"Confessions of an Economic Hit Man: How the U.S. Uses Globalization to Cheat Poor Countries Out of Trillions." Democracy Now! N.p. 9 Nov. 2004. Web. 31 Dec. 2016. <https://www.democracynow.org/2004/11/9/confessions_of_an_economic_hit_man>.

Copel, Lib. "Body Double: Both Sides Of the Ploy." The Washington Post. N.p. 21 March 2003. Web. 13 Jan. 2017. <https://www.washingtonpost.com/archive/lifestyle/2003/03/21/body-double-both-sides-of-the-ploy/8352f20e-2836-4896-891c-c686d8cd00de/>.

Cornwell, Rupert. "The Kim Jong-Il that Clinton Met Was a Fake, Says Academic." The Independent. N.p. 31 Oct. 2009. Web. 30 Dec. 2016. <http://www.independent.co.uk/news/world/asia/the-kim-jongil-that-clinton-met-was-a-fake-says-academic-1812286.html>.

Cornwell, Rupert. "The Saddam Conundrum: Was He Killed in First Raid?" The Independent. N.p. 22 March 2003. Web. 31 Dec. 2016. <http://www.independent.co.uk/news/world/middle-east/the-saddam-conundrum-was-he-killed-in-first-raid-111874.html>.

De La Garza, Paul. "The secrets behind the spies." St. Petersburg Times, N.p. 15 Aug. 2002. Web. 31 Dec. 2016. <http://www.sptimes.com/2002/08/15/Floridian/The_secrets_behind_th.shtml>.

Dean, Bradlee. "Politicians' Body Doubles Nothing New." WND. N.p. 15 Sept. 2016. Web. 30 Dec. 2016. <http://www.wnd.com/2016/09/politicians-body-doubles-nothing-new/>.

"De-Classified Document Admits Lee Harvey Oswald Was CIA." Federal Jack. Web. 31 Dec. 2016. <http://www.federaljack.com/de-classified-document-admits-lee-harvey-oswald-was-CIA/>.

"Definition of psyops." Merriam-webster.com. Web. 13 Jan. 2017. <https://www.merriam-webster.com/dictionary/psyops>.

Demick, Barbara. "A Dictator's Double Is Keeping Up Appearances." Los Angeles Times. N.p. 11 June 2006. Web. 30 Dec. 2016. <http://articles.latimes.com/2006/jun/11/world/fg-lookalike11/2>.

Di Fabio, Andriola and Alessandra Gigante. "Ask Who Was the 'Beatle.'" Wired Magazine. N.p. 15 July 2009. Web. 31 Dec. 2016. <http://plasticmacca.blogspot.com/2010/01/forensic-science-proves-paul-was.html>.

"Did Lee Harvey Oswald Kill J.D. Tippett?" 22November 1063. org.uk. Web. 9 Jan. 2017. <http://22november1963.org.uk/did-lee-harvey-oswald-kill-officer-jd-tippit>.

"Digital Forensics: Photo Tampering Throughout History [Slide Show]." Scientific American. N.p. 2 June 2008. Web. 31 Dec. 2016. <http://www.scientificamerican.com/slideshow.cfm?id=photo-tampering-throughout-history&%3Bphoto_id=4A94FA96-B59E-3711-A1F5658E0CEC8A7D>.

E., Ryan. "Stalin's Revision of History." Prezi.com. N.p. 3 Jan. 2013. Web. 31 Dec. 2016. <https://prezi.com/3vl7nrhgj9eg/stalins-revision-of-history/>.

El Mallah, Yasmeen, "Anis El-Dighidy." Egypt Today. N.p. May 2007. Web. 31 Dec. 2016. <http://web.archive.org/web/20070516071840/http://www.egypttoday.com/article.aspx?ArticleID=7376>.

"Face2Face: live video editing of facial expressions." Visage Technologies. N.p. 21 March 2016. Web. 9 Jan. 2017. <http://visagetechnologies.com/face2face-live-video-editing-of-facial-expressions/>.

"'Fake Photo' Revives Kim Rumours." BBC News. N.p. 12 Nov. 2008. Web. 31 Dec. 2016. <http://news.bbc.co.uk/2/hi/7715458.stm>.

Farid, Hany. "Seeing Is Not Believing." IEEE Spectrum: Technology, Engineering, and Science News. N.p. 31 July 2009. Web. 31 Dec. 2016. <http://spectrum.ieee.org/computing/software/seeing-is-not-believing/0>.

Fetzer, Jim and Jim Marrs. "JFK Assassination. False Flag Attacks: How 'Patsies' are Framed." Globalresearch.ca. N.p. 11 Dec. 2009. Web. 30 Dec. 2016. <http://www.globalresearch.ca/index.php?context=va&aid=16224>.

Freed, Dale Anne. "From jokester to jailbird." Toronto Star Thestar.com. N.p., 13 May 2007. Web. 30 Dec. 2016. <http://www.thestar.com/News/article/213298>.

"Frontline Transcript: Who Was Lee Harvey Oswald?" PBS. Air Date: 16 Nov. 16, 1993. Web. 31 Dec. 2016. <http://www.pbs.org/wgbh/frontline/film/oswald/transcript/>.

Goñi, Uki. "Tests on skull fragment cast doubt on Adolf Hitler suicide story." The Guardian. N.p. 26 Sept. 2009. Web. 15 Jan. 2017. <https://www.theguardian.com/world/2009/sep/27/adolf-hitler-suicide-skull-fragment>.

"Greatest Visual and Special Effects (F/X) - Milestones in Film." AMC Filmsite. Web. 5 Jan. 2017. <http://www.filmsite.org/visualeffects15.html>.

Harry, Ayana and Jesus Ayala. "Mask-Maker Rusty Slusser's Hollywood-Style Creations Fooled Cops, Airport Security." ABC News. N.p. 10 Dec. 2010. Web. 30 Dec. 2016. <http://abcnews.go.com/US/mask-maker-rusty-slussers-hollywood-style-face-coverings/story?id=12359536#.Ts3FeWA_ssE>.

Heckle, Harold. "Spanish lawmaker's photo used for bin Laden poster." Newsday. N.p. 16 Jan. 2010. Web. 31 Dec. 2016. <http://www.newsday.com/news/nation/spanish-lawmaker-s-photo-used-for-bin-laden-poster-1.1705738>.

Hildebrand, Holly. "The Mystery of Lee Harvey Oswald." The Houston Chronicle. N.p. 22 April 2000. Web. 30 Dec. 2016. <http://

web.archive.org/web/20000422222051/http://www.chron.com/content/chronicle/special/jfk/theory/oswald.html>.

Hill, Martin. "The Imposter General: Bernard Montgomery's D-Day Body Double." Decoded Past. N.p. 15 June 2013. Web. 30 Dec. 2016. <http://decodedpast.com/the-imposter-general-bernard-montgomerys-d-day-body-double/1332>.

Holloway, Henry. "'Putin is DEAD' Shock claims Vlad was killed YEARS ago and Russia led by 'body double.'" Daily Star Sunday. N.p. 24 Dec. 2016. Web. 1 Jan. 2017. <http://www.dailystar.co.uk/news/latest-news/572181/Vladimir-Putin-Russia-Body-Double-Dead-Poison-CIA-Mi6-Kremlin-US-Crimea>.

"Intcrview with the Assassin: Misinformaton." Magnolia Pictures. Web. 30 Dec. 2016. <http://web.archive.org/web/20021003185303/http://www.interviewwiththeassassin.com/misinformation.html>.

"Interview with the Assassin: Suspects." Magnolia Pictures. Web. 30 Dec. 2016. <http://web.archive.org/web/20021003185421/www.interviewwiththeassassin.com/suspects.html>.

"It's Not Saddam: A Story Calling for Investigation." Share International, N.p. 21 Dec. 2003. Web. 31 Dec. 2016. <http://www.globalresearch.ca/articles/CRG312B.html>.

"JFK Assassination Records: Findings." National Archives. Web. 11 Jan. 2017. <https://www.archives.gov/research/jfk/select-committee-report/part-1a.html>.

Jie-Ae, Sohn. "Meet Kim Jong Il's lookalike." CNN. Cable News Network. N.p. 7 Sept. 2006. Web. 30 Dec. 2016. <http://edition.cnn.com/2006/WORLD/asiapcf/09/07/kim.lookalike/index.html>.

"Jim Garrison: Interview with Playboy 9: Oswald and the FBI." 22november1963.org.uk. Web. 10 Jan. 2017. <http://22november1963.org.uk/jim-garrison-oswald-fbi>.

Kapnistos, Peter Fotis. "Soviet Autopsy: Hitler Died But His Double Escaped." GovernmentSecrets.com. N.p. 2014. Web. 31 Dec. 2016.

<http://www.governmentsecrets.com/soviet-autopsy-hitler-died-but-his-double-escaped/#>.

Kendrakahn. "How CGI technology allowed Forrest Gump to meet John F. Kennedy and John Lennon." Storify.com. Web. 5 Jan. 2017. <https://storify.com/kendrakahn/how-cgi-technology-allowed-forrest-gump-meet-john>.

"Kim Jong Il Photo A Fake, Report Claims." CBS News. N.p. 29 Jan. 2009. Web. 31 Dec. 2016. <http://www.cbsnews.com/stories/2009/06/29/world/main5122022.shtml>.

Kirk, Donald. "Did President Clinton meet N. Korea's Kim Jong-il or his look-alike?" The Christian Science Monitor. N.p. 29 Oct. 2009. Web. 30 Dec. 2016. <http://www.csmonitor.com/World/Asia-Pacific/2009/1029/p06s10-woap.html>.

Kirk, Donald. "Would the real Kim Jong-Il please sit back down in his wheelchair?" WorldTribune.com. N.p. 30 Oct. 2009. Web. 30 Dec. 2016. <http://www.worldtribune.com/worldtribune/WTARC/2009/ea_nkorea0848_10_30.asp>.

"Kirlian Photography." Altmd.com. Web. 31 Dec. 2016. <http://www.altmd.com/Articles/Kirlian-Photography--Encyclopedia-of-Alternative-M>.

Kitching, Chris. "Is this the greatest Hillary lookalike in the world? Advertising executive quit her job to impersonate the presidential candidate full-time." Daily Mail. N.p. 11 July 2016. Web. 7 Jan. 2017. <http://www.dailymail.co.uk/news/article-3684267/Hillary-Clinton-lookalike-Teresa-Barnwell-quit-job-impersonate-presidential-candidate-time.html>.

Knight, Katherine and Kelly Strange. "The 50-year-old mother who has spent £10,000 on surgery to look like her daughter," Daily Mail Online. N.p. 17 April 2009. Web. 31 Dec. 2016. <http://www.dailymail.co.uk/femail/article-1170348/The-50-year-old-mother-spent-10-000-surgery-look-like-daughter.html#ixzz0wdt9lqFM>.

Kotz, Pete. "Douglas Stewart Used Impostor to Derail Cops in Disappearance of Wife Venus Stewart." True Crime Report. N.p. 24 June 2010. Web. 11 Jan. 2017. <http://www.truecrimereport.com/2010/06/douglas_stewart_used_imposter.php>.

Kuchikomi. "N Korea's Kim Died in 2003; Replaced by Lookalike, Says Waseda Professor." Japan Today. N.p. 23 Aug. 2008. Web. 31 Dec. 2016. <https://www.japantoday.com/category/kuchikomi/view/north-koreas-kim-died-in-2003-and-was-replaced-by-lookalike-says-waseda-profesor>.

Kurtus, Ron. "Winston Churchill: Final Years (Ages 70 - 90).'"School for Champions. N.p. 6 Feb. 2006. Web. 31 Dec. 2016. <http://www.school-for-champions.com/biographies/winston_churchill_4.htm>.

Lane, Mark. *Plausible Denial: Was the CIA Involved in the Assassination of JFK?* New York: Thunder's Mouth Press, 1991. p. 64. Print.

Laytner, Ron. "The Man Who Makes Faces." Edit International. N.p. 2009. Web. 30 Dec. 2016. <http://web.archive.org/web/20120201021741/http://www.editinternational.com/read.php?id=47dddf8c807d1>.

Lipman, Masha. "Putin Disses Lenin." The New Yorker. N.p. 3 Sept. 2014. Web. 17 Jan. 2017. <http://www.newyorker.com/news/news-desk/putin-disses-lenin>.

MacKinnon, Mark. "Iraqis doubt real Hussein behind bars." The Globe and Mail. N.p. 18 Dec. 2003. Web. 31 Dec. 2016. <http://www.theglobeandmail.com/news/world/iraqis-doubt-real-hussein-behind-bars/article1170845/>.

Mansfield, Katie. "Secret FBI files 'reveal Hitler DID fake death' after WW2 then flew to TENERIFE." Daily Express. N.p. 8 Jan. 2016. Web. 31 Dec. 2016. <http://www.express.co.uk/news/weird/632677/Adolf-Hitler-Nazi-fake-death-World-War-Two-Tenerife>.

Marino, James F. "The FBI Psychological Operation & The Go Betweens Who Furtively Carry Out The FBI's Psychological

Warfare Operations." The Mother of All Black Ops. N.p. 30 Sept. 2011. Web. 5 Jan. 2017. <http://9-11themotherofallblackoperations.blogspot.com/2011/09/fbi-psychological-operation-go-betweens.html>.

Marrs, Jim. "[Marrs Jim] Crossfire, The Plot That Killed Kenned (BookZa.org).HTML." Docshare.tips. N.p. June 2016. Web. 30 Dec. 2016. <http://docshare.tips/marrs-jim-crossfire-the-plot-that-killed-kennedbookzaorghtml_576c5fe8b6d87f8a3c8b4953.html?utm_source=docshare&utm_medium=sidebar&utm_campaign=5758c141b6d87fa8218b45c7>.

May, Ashley. "The Internet thinks Hillary Clinton has a body double." USA Today. N.p. 13 Sept. 2016. Web. 30 Dec. 2016. <http://www.usatoday.com/story/news/nation-now/2016/09/13/internet-thinks-hillary-clinton-has-body-double/90297312/>.

May, Stephen. "The Top 10 Impostors in Fiction." The Guardian. N.p. 12 March 2014. Web. 2 Jan. 2017. <https://www.theguardian.com/books/2014/mar/12/top-10-impostors-fiction-stephen-may>.

McCombs, Phil. "Crafting Hope." Washington Post. N.p. 12 Jan. 2003. Web. 30 Dec. 2016. <http://www.washingtonpost.com/wp-dyn/content/article/2007/05/22/AR2007052201310_5.html>.

McWethy, John, Brian Ross, Pierre Thomas and Martha Raddatz. "Saddam Hit? U.S.: Saddam Seen Leaving Baghdad Complex on a Gurney After Strike." ABC News. N.p. 21 March 2003. Web. 31 Dec. 2016. <http://web.archive.org/web/20030324225555/http://abcnews.go.com/sections/world/World/iraq_saddam_030321.html>.

McWethy, John and Brian Ross, Pierre Thomas and Martha Raddatz. "U.S. Officials: Saddam Seen on Gurney." ABC News. N.p. 21 March 2003. Web. 31 Dec. 2016. <http://abcnews.go.com/International/story?id=79614&page=1>.

Moore, Malcolm and Julian Ryall. "North Korea Denies Kim Jong-Il Dead and Claim 'Conspiracy.'" The Telegraph. N.p. 10 Sept. 2008. Web. 31 Dec. 2016. <http://www.telegraph.co.uk/news/2775598/North-Korea-deny-Kim-Jong-il-dead-and-claim-conspiracy.html>

Morales, Tatiana. "CIA: Man On Tape Is Saddam." CBS News. N.p. 21 March 2003. Web. 30 Dec. 2016. <http://www.cbsnews.com/stories/2003/03/20/eveningnews/main544812.shtml>.

"November 22: The Evidence." J.D. Tippett. Web. 9 Jan. 2017. <https://www.jdtippit.com/evidence_nov.htm>.

Nikita Khrushchev Quotes." Web. 17 Jan. 2017. <http://www.azquotes.com/author/7985-Nikita_Khrushchev>.

O'Flynn, Elaine. "What has he been Putin on his face? How Russian leader Vladimir's appearance has changed dramatically through the years and he looks younger than ever." Daily Mail. N.p. 16 April 2015. Web. 1 Jan. 2017. <http://www.dailymail.co.uk/news/article-3042134/What-Putin-face-Russian-leader-Vladimirs-appearance-changed-dramatically-years-looks-younger-ever.html>.

Osborn, Andrew. "Adolf Hitler suicide story questioned after tests reveal skull is a woman's." The Telegraph. N.p. 28 Sept. 2009. Web. 15 Jan. 2017. <http://www.telegraph.co.uk/history/world-war-two/6237028/Adolf-Hitler-suicide-story-questioned-after-tests-reveal-skull-is-a-womans.html>.

"Oswald the Impostor." JFK Lancer. Web. 30 Dec. 2016. <http://www.jfklancer.com/Page4.html>.

"Our Process." Facefirst.com. Web. 4 Jan. 2017. <http://www.facefirst.com/how-it-works/our-process>.

Pelton, Robert Young. "Iraq - President Saddam Hussein al-Tikriti." N.p. 2000. Web. 31 Dec. 2016. <http://web.archive.org/web/20010504000910/http://www.comebackalive.com/df/dplaces/iraq/player5.htm>.

"Phantomas Elaborate Face Recognition." Global-security-solutions.com. Web. 4 Jan. 2017. <http://web.archive.org/web/20090329102843/http://www.global-security-solutions.com/FaceRecognition.htm>.

"Pieces of the Puzzle: Great Moments in the Conspiracy Timeline." Texas Monthly. N.p. Nov. 1983. Web. 30 Dec. 2016. p. 156. <http://www.texasmonthly.com/articles/pieces-of-the-puzzle/>.

Pierce v. Dep't of the United States Air Force, 512 F.3d 184, 188 (5th Cir. Miss. 2007).

Pike, John. "FM 90-2: Battlefield Deception CHAPTER 5 Deception Means." Web. 30 Dec. 2016. <http://www.globalsecurity.org/intell/library/policy/army/fm/90-2/90-2ch5.htm>.

Pogodin, Maxim. "Saddam's wife could not recognize her husband." Pravda.ru. N.p. 13 April 2004. Web. 31 Dec. 2016. <http://web.archive.org/web/20040606051747/http://english.pravda.ru/world/20/91/366/12494_saddam.html>.

Poole-Robb, Stuart. "How cyber criminals are embracing voice morphing." ITProPortal. N,p. 9 Oct. 2015. Web. 13 Jan. 2017. <http://www.itproportal.com/2015/10/09/how-cyber-criminals-are-embracing-voice-morphing/>.

"Psychological Warfare." Allexperts. com. Web. 30 Dec. 2016. <http://web.archive.org/web/20080709014354/http://en.allexperts.com/e/p/ps/psychological_warfare.htm>.

"Radio-Vision: Scientific Milestone." Drown Laboratories. N.p. 1960. Web. 31 Dec. 2016. <http://educate-yourself.org/tjc/radiovisionbookintro30jul03.shtml>.

Rahman, Md. Mahbubur, et al. "Person Identification Using Ear Biometrics." International Journal of the Computer, the Internet and Management, Vol. 15#2 (May-Aug. 2007), pp. 1-8. Web. 4 Jan. 2017. <http://www.journal.au.edu/ijcim/2007/may07/IJCIMvol15no2_article1.pdf>.

Rao, Nathan. "Hitler DID escape Germany in 1945: Staggering new claims point to huge Nazi cover-up." Daily Express. N.p. 12 June 2015. Web. 31 Dec. 2016. <http://www.express.co.uk/news/weird/583845/Did-Hitler-ESCAPE-Germany-in-1945-Staggering-new-discovery-points-to-huge-Nazi-cover-up>.

"Rashid, Josef Stalin's stand-in." Associated Press. St. Petersburg Times. 17 June 1991 (7B).

Recknagel, Charles. "Iraq: Seeing Double In Baghdad -- Saddam Uses Look-Alikes To Disguise His Whereabouts." Radio Free Europe/Radio Liberty. N.p. 9 Oct. 2002. Web. 31 Dec. 2016. <http://www.rferl.org/content/article/1101033.html>.

Rosenbaum, Ron. "Still on the Case." Texas Monthly. N.p. Nov. 1983. Web. 30 Dec. 2016. p. 270. <http://www.texasmonthly.com/politics/still-on-the-case/>.

Ross, Bernie. "Training SOE Saboteurs in World War Two." BBC News. N.P. 17 Feb. 2011. Web. 31 Dec. 2016. <http://www.bbc.co.uk/history/worldwars/wwtwo/soe_training_01.shtml>.

Ryall, Julian. "Kim Jong-Il 'died in 2003', says Japanese professor." The Telegraph. 7 Sept. 2008. Web. 31 Dec. 2016. <http://www.telegraph.co.uk/news/2699670/Kim-Jong-Il-died-in-2003-says-Japanese-professor.html>.

"Saddam's 'Double' Trouble." WND. N.p. 26 March 2003. Web. 31 Dec. 2016. <http://www.wnd.com/2003/03/17941/>.

"Saddam's 'Double' Trouble: Opposition Leader Claims Hussein Died Of Cancer In 1999." Rense.com. N.p. 26 Mar. 2003. Web. 14 Aug. 2019. <http://www.rense.com/general46/doub.htm>.

"Scelso," John. "HSCA Security Classified Testimony: I-33." Historymatters.com. N.p. 16 May 1978. Web. 30 Dec. 2016. <http://www.history-matters.com/archive/jfk/hsca/secclass/Scelso_5-16-78/html/Scelso_0037a.htm>.

"Scelso," John. "HSCA Security Classified Testimony: I-37." Historymatters.com. N.p. 16 May 1978. Web. 4 Jan. 2017. <http://www.history-matters.com/archive/jfk/hsca/secclass/Scelso_5-16-78/html/Scelso_0041a.htm>.

"Scelso," John. "HSCA Security Classified Testimony: 1-44." 16 May 1978. Web. 30 Dec. 2016. <http://www.history-matters.com/ archive/jfk/hsca/secclass/Scelso_5-16-78/html/Scelso_0048a.htm>.

"Scelso," John. "HSCA Security Classified Testimony: 1-59." Historymatters.com. N.p. 16 May 1978. Web. 30 Dec. 2016. <http:// www.history-matters.com/archive/jfk/hsca/secclass/Scelso_5-16-78/ html/Scelso_0063a.htm>.

"Scelso," John. "HSCA Security Classified Testimony: 1-123." Historymatters.com. N.p. 16 May 1978. Web. 30 Dec. 2016. <http:// www.history-matters.com/archive/jfk/hsca/secclass/Scelso_5-16-78/ html/Scelso_0128a.htm>.

"Scelso," John. "HSCA Security Classified Testimony: 1-160." Historymatters.com. N.p. 16 May 1978. Web. 30 Dec. 2016. <http:// www.history-matters.com/archive/jfk/hsca/secclass/Scelso_5-16-78/ html/Scelso_0164a.htm>.

"Scelso," John. "HSCA Security Classified Testimony: 1-173." Historymatters.com. N.p. 16 May 1978. Web. 30 Dec. 2016. <http:// www.history-matters.com/archive/jfk/hsca/secclass/Scelso_5-16-78/ html/Scelso_0177a.htm>.

"Scelso," John. "HSCA Security Classified Testimony: 1-178." Historymatters.com. N.p. 16 May 1978. Web. 30 Dec. 2016. <http:// www.history-matters.com/archive/jfk/hsca/secclass/Scelso_5-16-78/ html/Scelso_0182a.htm>.

Sheridan, Michael. "North Korea 'uses doubles to hide death of Kim.'" The Sunday Times. N.p. 7 Sept. 2008. Web. 31 Dec. 2016. <http://web.archive.org/web/20080911065831/http:// www.timesonline.co.uk/tol/news/world/asia/article4692472.ece>.

Shipman, Claire. "'Master of Disguise' Changes Many Lives." ABC News. N.p. 29 Nov. 2005. Web. 30 Dec. 2016. <http:// abcnews.go.com/Health/Cosmetic/story?id=1354130>.

Sivaraman, K. "Voice Morphing." International Journal of Computer Trends and Technology (IJCTT) – volume 3 Issue 1 Number 3 – Jan 2012. Web. 13. Jan. 2017. <http://

www.ijcttjournal.org/Volume3/issue-1/number-3/IJCTT-V3I1N3P3.pdf>.

Sloan, Tim. "Ex-CIA Disguise Master Helps Disfigured People." Sawfnews.com. N.p. 11 Dec. 2005. Web. 30 Dec. 2016. <http://web.archive.org/web/20100721123311/http://www.sawfnews.com/lifestyle/4825.aspx>.

Solsman, Joan E. "Samsung deepfake AI could fabricate a video of you from a single profile pic. Even the Mona Lisa can be faked." CNet. N.p. 24 May 2019. Web. 14 Aug. 2019. <https://www.cnet.com/news/samsung-ai-deepfake-can-fabricate-a-video-of-you-from-a-single-photo-mona-lisa-cheapfake-dumbfake/?fbclid=IwAR0V7szeAaTFvAImel8FBplbWXT9Cvv-KTUU06NxMI0cdHU8LktNwj7kJBk>.

Springmeier, Fritz. *Deeper insight into the Illuminati Formula*. Charleston, SC: Createspace, 2010. p. 312. Print.

Stein, Jeff. "CIA unit's wacky idea: Depict Saddam as gay." The Washington Post. N.p. 25 May 2010. Web. 31 Dec. 2016. <http://web.archive.org/web/20101118063712/http://blog.washingtonpost.com/spy-talk/2010/05/cia_group_had_wacky_ideas_to_d.html>.

Stewart, Will. "The man who was Stalin's body double finally tells his story." Daily Mail Online. N.p. 12 April 2008.. Web. 30 Dec. 2016. <http://www.dailymail.co.uk/news/article-559234/The-man-Stalins-body-double-finally-tells-story.html>.

"Strike on Iraq: Interview With Graham Fuller." N.p. 20 March 2003. Web. 17 Jan. 2017. <http://transcripts.cnn.com/TRANSCRIPTS/0303/20/se.19.html>.

Takahashi, Kosuke. "Seeing Doubles in Dear Leader's No-Show." Asia Times. N.p. 10 Sept. 2008. Web. 31 Dec. 2016. <http://www.atimes.com/atimes/Korea/JI10Dg01.html>.

"Text of Interview with John Loftus." MSNBC. N.p. 25 July 2003. Web. 31 Dec. 2016. <http://www.globalresearch.ca/articles/CRG312B.html>.

"5 Reasons Julian Assange Interview with John Pilger is FAKE? #WhereisAssange #ProofOfLife." The Outer Dark. N.p. 3 Dec. 2016. Web. 5 Jan. 2016. <https://www.youtube.com/watch?v=anbn3kFL17k>.

"The Secrets of the U.S. Election: Julian Assange Talks to John Pilger." Johnpilger.com. N.p. 5 Nov. 2016. Web. 6 Jan. 2017. <http://johnpilger.com/articles/the-secrets-of-the-us-election-julian-assange-talks-to-john-pilger>.

Thies, Justus, et al. "Face2Face Real Time Face Capture and Reenactment of RGB Videos." Graphics.stanford.edu. N.p. June 2016. Web. 5 Jan. 2017. <http://www.graphics.stanford.edu/~niessner/thies2016face.html>.

Thorpe, Vanessa. "Finest hour for actor who was Churchill's radio voice." The Observer. Guardian News and Media. N.p. 29 Oct. 2000. Web. 30 Dec. 2016. <https://www.theguardian.com/media/2000/oct/29/uknews.theobserver>.

United States v. Hawes, 523 F.3d 245, 249 (3d Cir. Pa. 2008).

United States v. Mitchell, 518 F.3d 230 (4th Cir. S.C. 2008).

Vialls, Joe. "Mrs Saddam says Saddam is not Saddam." Propagandamatrix.com. N.p. 18 June 2004. Web. 31 Dec. 2016. <http://www.propagandamatrix.com/articles/june2004/180604saddamnotsaddam.htm>.

Vialls, Joe. "Shaddam Shaddam's New Vaudeville Scam!" Joevialls.altermedia.info. N.p. 3 July 2004. Web. 31 Dec. 2016. <http://web.archive.org/web/20040704142248/http://joevialls.altermedia.info/iraq/vaudeville.html>.

"Vladimir Putin accuses Lenin of placing a 'time bomb' under Russia." The Guardian. N.p. 25 Jan. 2016. Web. 17 Jan. 2017. <https://www.theguardian.com/world/2016/jan/25/vladmir-putin-accuses-lenin-of-placing-a-time-bomb-under-russia>.

"Voice Verification." Globalsecurity.org. Web. 4 Jan. 2017. <http://www.globalsecurity.org/security/systems/biometrics-voice.htm>. Vronsky, Peter. "Lee Harvey Oswald in Russia An Unauthorized History from the Kennedy Assassination." Russianbooks.org. Web. 31 Dec. 2016. <http://www.russianbooks.org/oswald/discrep.htm>.

Wallace, Robert and H. Keith Melton. *Spycraft*. USA: Dutton, 2008. p. 387. Print.

"Was Oswald an FBI Agent?" 22november1963.org.uk. Web. 9 Jan. 2017. <http://22november1963.org.uk/memo-was-oswald-an-fbi-agent>.

Whaley, Barton and Susan Stratton Aykroyd. *Turnabout and Deception: Crafting the Double-Cross and the Theory of Outs.* Annapolis, MD: Naval Institute Press, 2016. p. 66.

"What is Biometrics." IGI Global. Web. 31 Dec. 2016. <http://www.igi-global.com/dictionary/biometrics/2542>.

"What is Facial Recognition?" Facefirst.com. Web. 3 Jan. 2017. <ttp://www.facefirst.com/how-it-works>.

"What Was Lee Harvey Oswald's Alibi?" 22november1963.org.uk. Web. 10 Jan. 2017. <http://22november1963.org.uk/lee-harvey-oswald-alibi>.

"Who Saw Lee Harvey Oswald in the TSBD Sixth-Floor Window?" 22november1963.org.uk. Web. 10 Jan. 2017. <http://22november1963.org.uk/who-saw-oswald-in-the-sixth-floor-window>.

Zeller, Tom. "The World; Will the Real Saddam Hussein Please Step Down." The New York Times. N.p. 6 Oct. 2002. Web. 30 Dec. 2016. <http://www.nytimes.com/2002/10/06/weekinreview/the-world-will-the-real-saddam-hussein-please-step-down.html>.